RIVER FRIEND

A series of Riverine Small Books

by Sylvia M. Haslam and Tina Bone

BOOK 7

WATER—Clean and Dirty

Bath, Somerset—Roman baths originally built between 60 and 70 AD

Seventh published book in the Series:

WATER—Clean and Dirty

A Book in a series of Riverine publications by

Sylvia M. Haslam and Tina Bone

(Each book is about a different subject so the series can be read in any order)

Written and Edited by Sylvia Haslam and Tina Bone. Illustrated by Tina Bone (unless otherwise stated)

(Special thanks to Russell Biggs whose very graphic photographs of pollution in Norfolk taken in January 2022 shown in Fig. 1 of this Book, are a much valued contribution.)

RFS7: PAPERBACK **66** pp.
ISBN No. 978 1 9162096 7 1
98 Illustrations

Published by: Tina Bone UK
First edition: **July 2022**

https://riverfriend.tinasfineart.uk
Email: ourbooks@tinasfineart.uk

CONTENTS

INTRODUCTION TO THE SERIES

Rivers are vital. They bring freshwater to the land, on which all its life depends. They are beautiful and fascinating, making up both the typical British countryside and many of its most spectacular views. If they vanished, what hardship and outrage there would be! Yet, slowly, slowly, they are vanishing, the larger stream becomes smaller, the tiny brook becomes a ditch and dries, and is filled in— the small ditches get polluted and dug out, become dull, and vanish from sight and consciousness. How can we save our rivers and riverscapes? How can we raise awareness on this slow, almost invisible loss?

We believe that this series of handy, small books, suitable for readers from teenage upwards, will help to raise awareness. Individually, each book tells a story on a particular riverine and riparian environment. Collectively, the series will inform, in a simple and effective manner, the extraordinary value of freshwater and its plants.

The Authors realised that there was a huge gap in the literature. There are many publications for scientists, for pond-dippers, birders and anglers, but "easy-read" books focussing on the river itself, and the vegetation belonging to it and creating the habitat for all else: we could find none!

For explanations regarding British freshwater plants, terminology mentioned throughout the series, and Picture Guide and reference section for further reading, see the book entitled *A PROLOGUE TO THE SERIES: Plant identification and Glossary of Terms* (also available to view in pdf format free on-line at https://riverfriend.tinasfineart.uk/resources/)

Other titles in the Series are listed on the last page of this book and on the River Friend Website:
https://riverfriend.tinasfineart.uk

WATER—Clean and Dirty

Introduction

Each book in the "RIVER FRIEND" series deals with or introduces some aspect of rivers and their waters. This book is about the chemical nature of the water, clean or dirty, and also what this does to the plants which might—or do—grow in it.

Water. River. The majestic Thames, the rushing mighty Tweed or (Aberdeen) Dee, the rippling peaty stream or burn, the quiet meandering brook. Rivers all over the place. And the near-black smelly water of the industrial river (despite all efforts, not yet right, but slowly, progress is being made), and the unexpected bright blue (dye), red (dye), or even white (paper?) water which is so striking, even if so polluted. River water *fairly clean, moderately polluted,* and *awful*—all over the place (see Fig. 1 1–29).

Pollution entering, top left, into stream already polluted

Surface-polluted foam (detergent) blown by wind. Stream water brown–turbid–polluted

Look at the colours! Gross pollution entering a Chalkstream stream in Norfolk January 2022 (Photographs, courtesy of Russell Biggs, @RussellB1ggs). No even edge vegetation

Rubbish and polluted run-off in a backwater stream in Norfolk, February 2022 (Photographs, courtesy of Russell Biggs, @RussellB1ggs)

*Further downstream of **5-6**, February 2022 (Photographs, courtesy of Russell Biggs, @RussellB1ggs)*

Oil, sewage, chemical, and silt pollution. Despite this, there are a few water plants.

Yellowing foliage is diagnostic for mild organic
pollution

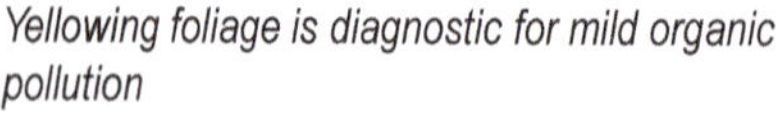

Heavy silt layer covering aquatic plants

Duckweed (Lemna minor) (13) is a British native flora species, but "aliens" such as Water-fern (Azolla, magnified inset) (14), and large-leaved Floating Pennywort (Hydrocotyle ranunculoides) (15) disrupt by disturbing the natural balance of a river

Alien fauna such as the American signal crayfish (Pacifastacus leniusculus) (16) also disrupt: here being caught by holding on to bacon bait and refusing to let go!

17 
18
19

17–28. Lovely clear water in different types of stream might still be polluted. 17. Lowland Chalkstream, Norfolk. Over-silted (rib-pattern in red circle) and unstable substrate, chemical and physical balance destroyed, over-shaded. This combination of impacts eliminates aquatic plants. Note the slight grey tinge—characteristic of near-clean chalk water; 18. Highland stream, Cumbria; 19. Water from a Chalkhill spring, Bassingbourn, Cambridgeshire; 20. Lowland clay stream, Bourn Brook, Cambridgeshire; 21. Clear hill stream at the bottom of Mamtor, Derbyshire; 22. River Wye Monsal Trail—lots of wild garlic and mosses; 23. River Wye Monsal Trail—natural debris and good animal habitat; 24. Lovely walk along the River Wye with Monsal Trail viaduct above; 25. Dovedale—natural weir along the River Dove (too shallow!); 26. Clear, cold water surrounding the middle-river island full of Wood anemones (Anemone nemorosa), River Dove, early April 2022; 27. River Wye near the Monsal Trail, spring Ranunculus (almost too shallow); 28. River Wye upstream of 27, showing abundant Butterbur (Petasites hybridus) and Watercress (Rorippa nasturtium-aquaticum) in clear waters

Compare details of "clean" foam here—and 18, 19, 27—with the detergent foam in 1, 2, 5, 7, 8, 9

Even clear water varies. There is the almost shiny-clear of the Chalkstream (17) (limestone), the brown-clear of the peaty moorland stream (21), the often-dull (not quite clear) of the clay stream (20), and many more. Clear? Please note that unfortunately there is an easy but sadly false association in all our minds that clear water is clean. This is not so. In Britain little or no stream water is clean. Even in a remote place, who can be sure a dead sheep does not lurk upstream behind that far corner? And worse.*

Waters are turbid too—looking down, the bottom is not visible, whether it be 5cm or 5m down. Some turbidity is natural, for example, storms erode soil and the silty water swirls downriver and may take a couple of days or so to clear after rain. Fine particles of clay tend to hang around, particularly in winter when rain (so erosion) is more, and slight turbidity results. The clearest water is seen in limestone springs in excellent habitats in North America, where the bottom (and its plants) are visible at 5–6m down. *"And its plants"*—plants need light for life and growth, and most clean(ish) streams, however clear the water, have very little light below 2m. (This does have its uses: river vegetation extends only a little deeper.)

The more turbid waters, where beds cannot be seen deeper than 75cm or so, are generally so because they are polluted. Most often they are some variety of grey-brown, but the water can be any colour. This may be mostly soil, where mis-management has made streams more liable to erosion, and silt and clay are washed out in excess. It may also be dirty run-off from cultivation. Bare soil encourages erosion and just think what farmers need to put on their fields! Agrochemicals (fertilizers, pesticides) of various kinds. And what about the unwanted parts of crops (often roots) that just stay on the fields?

Run-off from roads contains many "nasties". After a week or so with no rain, run-off water is very dark, even near-black: rubber, bitumen, other tyre derivatives, heavy metals, petrochemicals and other hydrocarbons from exhaust fumes, petrol, diesel and oil, glass, aggregate derivatives from tarmac, showers, de-icing salt (winter), dead leaves, stems (branches) and animals,

---

*A note from Sylvia Haslam: "I once took water samples from about 500 streams scattered around England—in lowland, hills, remote places, towns— Nearly ALL contained detergent, in varying quantities. Detergent was chosen as being quite easy to test for, and a substance which does not come alone. Can you think of a reason—bar the odd child playing—why anyone should put just detergent in to a river? No? Nor could I! Detergent is household waste and, where there is detergent, there is sewage and washing water. It is surprising how much gets everywhere."

spills from any type of load, and fire-fighting chemicals. A toxic cocktail indeed. But now everyone is so used to it—and it looks just like soil—that hardly any one thinks of it. Yet traffic increases every year.

There is much pollution from specific sources. Point sources include factories, farms, car parks, large roads, and so on. These also have very varied chemicals (Fig. 1 29)!

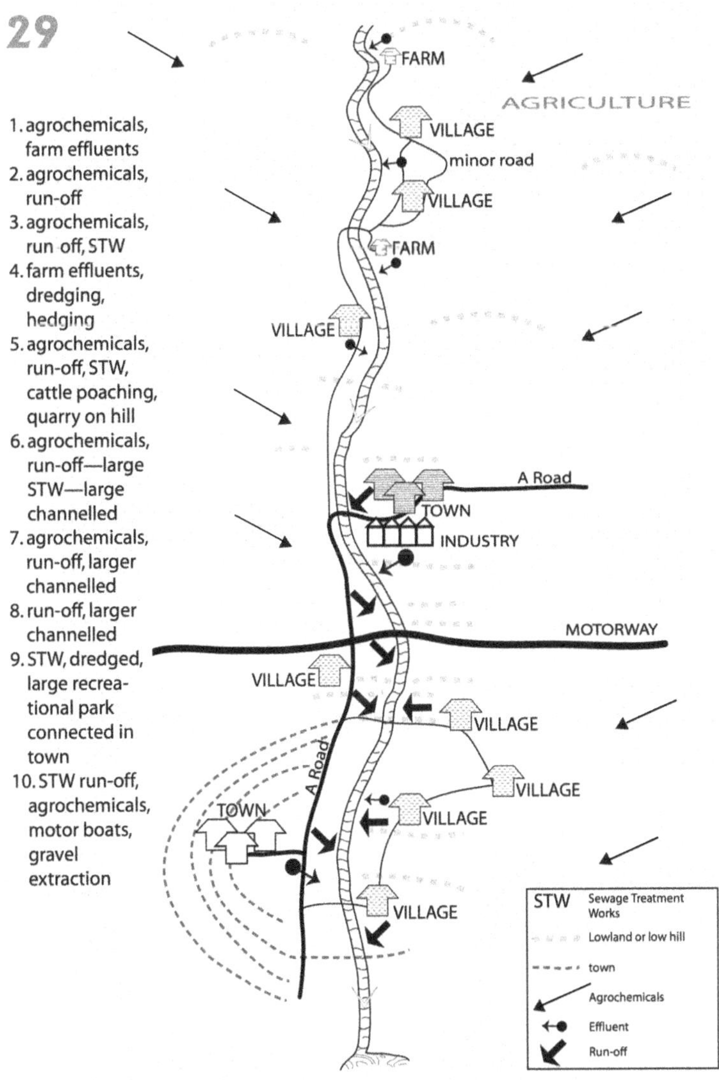

Ten examples of Cumulative Pollution

Where water comes from

What is clean water? Is it pure water, water with nothing else, nothing added, nothing dissolved in it, nothing picked up on the way? No, not in Britain anyway! And never since humans arrived! Nor would pure water be good for the plants and animals living within it! Rain falls from clouds, and may pick up a little material there (for example, sulphuric acid from some heavy-industry factories, as happened in the Peak District in the nineteenth century, or, more recently, ammonia from Dutch pig farms). Normally much more important is what the rainwater picks up *after* it lands. Surfaces bear chemicals which can be, and are, washed out—washed off—by rain. (A good shower cleans cars well!) The chemicals vary with the surface: road run-off, bare soil, blanket bog, coniferous forest, deciduous oak forest, arable, maize (sweetcorn), vegetables, and so on. As rain becomes run-off it takes on a chemical character which reflects the surfaces through which it has passed. The principal sources of this character are the soil and the rock below, from which the soil is, typically, derived. Of course, as in all ecology, there are exceptions. In Britain the largest exception is where glacial deposit, boulder clay, sits on top of another rock type, say chalk or sandstone, and nearly all the chemical influence is from the clay.

Rain falls on the land, runs off the land, gathers into rills, which gather into brooks, rivers, and finally it ends up in the sea. Some rainwater is evaporated back into the air before that end, more is transpired (evaporated) from the vegetation, and in porous or cavernous rock, water sinks right down into rock, forming aquifers. Aquifer water may, as in Bath, Somerset (Fig. 2), be ten thousand years old, or it may be very recent, more accurately termed "flush-water" or "storm-water", running straight to the stream only a little below ground level.

Either way, and as just mentioned above, the composition of stream water reflects that of the material it has flowed through. Hence the very different nature of, say, a Chalkstream and a blanket-bog stream. This is not just shown in extremes. The two main British types of lowland soft limestone streams, chalk and oolite, have different plant assemblages. Not very different though, as chalk and oolite are not very different, but nonetheless they are different. The oolite usually contains a little clay, whose run-off water—inherent nutrients—is more nutrient-rich, and less skewed towards calcium dominance, and the vegetation (species assemblages) normally reflects this.

Fig. 2. The Roman baths, Bath. Over time, water from the Mendip Hills percolates many metres through limestone aquifers. Geothermal energy far below ground heats the water from 69° to 96°C and this bubbles to the surface via thermal springs

Clean river water, therefore, is not pure water. It differs greatly from distilled water which (in sterile conditions) is "pure" water. Clean river water is that where there is no human interference to the chemical status of the catchment land, or river proper. Which is to say, there is none in Britain or, now, anywhere else in the world! The best that can be found is where such human interference is least—parts of, say, Greenland. There does remain, however, a great difference between remote parts of highland Britain (where human interference is low), between rock types such as limestone, sandstone, and clay, and between ordinary agricultural lowlands, and built-up towns and cities—where other chemical influences are added to these.

What is in Water?

A major hurdle to the study of water is that no one knows exactly what is in it. No sample has ever been analysed, not spring water, not bog water, not Thames water, not even water from the tap. Of course the major nutrients are well known, calcium, phosphorus, nitrogen and the like, and pesticides spread on the land are reasonably well known from analyses of the rivers they pass into. But it is hardly an exaggeration to say 100,000 minor organic and inorganic chemicals have been identified from water (not all in the same sample, of course!). Humus-related elements—dead leaf, stem and animal remains—have received little of the attention they deserve. It is easy to say "Surely they are inert?", but how many substances are? And at what concentrations do they influence the river, either in themselves or by their interaction with other substances?

However authoritatively scientists manage to write about water chemicals, the extent of the *unknown—"the known unknowns and the unknown unknowns"* (to quote the 2002 American saying by Donald H. Rumsfeld)—is major. Not just in trace concentrations, either. It is only in the past decade or two that the large amounts of methane in Chalkstreams has become known. Methane? Yes, a well-known gas, which reacts with other chemicals, and is obvious once looked for. But previously no one thought to look for it! What else? When **Total Dissolved Solids** are measured, river water typically contains 300–400ppm (parts per million). All the measured chemicals together come to maybe 30–40ppm. Just around 10% of what is known to be there, 90% is unaccounted for. That is a good measure of the *"Unknowns"*!

Samuel Taylor Coleridge wrote a poem about Cologne in the early nineteenth century which well illustrates how town pollution works:

> In Köhln, a town of monks and bones,
> And pavements fang'd with murderous stones
> [*dodgy pavements are not just recent!*]
> And rags, and hags, and hideous wenches;
> I counted two and seventy stenches,
> All well defined, and several stinks!
> Ye Nymphs that reign o'er sewers and sinks
> The River Rhine, it is well known,
> Doth wash your city of Cologne;
> But tell me, Nymphs, what power divine
> Shall henceforth wash the River Rhine?

Squalor means dirt. Dirt means pollution, and, before Sewage Treatment Works (STW), much river-town dirt went into the river (regulations varied with town, country and period). Indeed, how could the Rhine be cleaned by cleaning Cologne? It could not. Now there are Sewage Treatment Works: some good, some bad or ineffective, some making a major difference to the pollution. (See the book in this Series: *Vegetation Changes Over Time. Is there*

14

FREEZE FRAME? for the story of the Aberdeen Don, which had a STW hardly affecting the river vegetation, despite receiving a lot of domestic and minor industrial pollution.)

Rock type, soil type and nutrient status

What are these? The rock type is what the land is made of down below the surface (Fig. 3). A river's whole catchment may be one rock type, or it may be two, or more, and where there are several, they may be layered vertically, as with glacial clay overlying chalk, or separated horizontally, as when a river rises on chalk and, further downstream, flows on to clay, or it may be both. But where streams or rivers run, they run through the rock and are influenced by its type. Roughly speaking, the more of a catchment is covered by, has streams flowing over and in a rock type, the stronger the influence of this rock type on both the character and chemical composition of the stream. When a stream flows from one to another, at their junction all the river water is that of the upstream rock. Further down, the land, so (typically) the run-off water, is of the second rock type, and so are any tributaries entering the main river from that part of the catchment. It can therefore be some miles downstream of the junction before the vegetation takes on the characters of the second rock type.

Some interesting patterns result. For instance, when a clay stream flows on to chalk, the water continues to be "clayey" until there is considerable chalk influence. The bed of the river, though, is still clay or gravel. This moves in the river much more slowly than the water itself and it is only a few miles that these clay particles are carried downstream anyway. Where there is shallow clay soil over chalk (or vice versa) both can be found, one mostly in the upper soil layer, the other in the lower layer. With these niches of double-chemical status, for roots, site diversity may be much enhanced. Instead of, say, 8 species, there may be 13 or even 18 in around 20m of stream length. (The same increased diversity may be found near the sea, where both mild and moderately brackish (salty) conditions may be found together.)

Where one rock-type is more nutrient-rich than the other, as when passing from resistant (low nutrient) to old red sandstone (high nutrient), then the higher nutrient rock has the stronger influence.

Soil type (river-bed substrate type) is basically derived from the rock below but there are various complicating factors. Where bog peat has developed over,

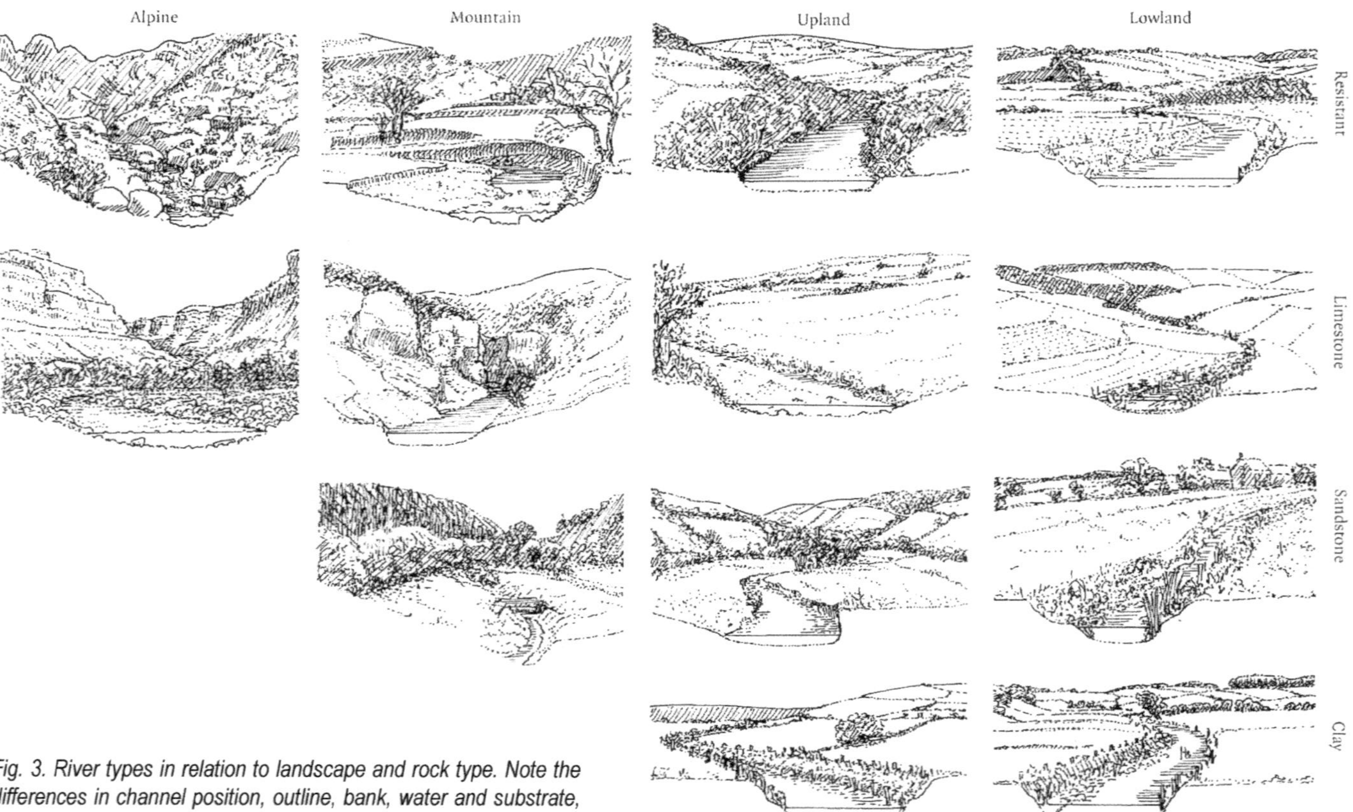

Fig. 3. River types in relation to landscape and rock type. Note the differences in channel position, outline, bank, water and substrate, and in the vegetation diversity and cover. (Illustration by Y Bower)

for example, moorland, this is nutrient-low with the peculiar constituents of this peat, which run off into the streams with the rainwater. The importance of this to the river may be total when Blanket Bog peat is the only chemical influence on the stream, or negligible, or anything in between. A thin layer of desert sand blown—in past ages—on to chalk in part of Western France means the river vegetation is (depending on the point of view!) contaminated, or enhanced, by adding sandstone influence to the chalk, and so on. This is known, provided time permits, by recording the river vegetation of just-Chalkstreams and using them as a reference standard for the mixed ones.

There are the bits of soil that fall in too, which, if they dissolve (disintegrate) in the water, influence it chemically—or not much. Under trees, many leaves drop on the water, or are washed into the water. Birch and conifer have a slight nutrient-poor influence. Most of the rest are more nutrient-rich. Soil washed in, if unpolluted, has the same effect as the same soil on the banks. Soil already influenced, for instance, by road dirt adds that particular pollution. Wood is valuable as animal habitat, but also as plant habitat, and recent improvement schemes often include placing tree branches or indeed larger bits of trees strategically to increase habitat variation, decrease erosion and slow down the flow of water.

Where traditional vegetation is present (from flower-rich meadow to oak wood to alpine grassland), run-off (so stream water) varies with the vegetation type. An equally great variation comes within crops, but here the run-off varies also, and varies more with the agrichemicals put on the land. Different crops are given different amounts of fertilizer at different times, and a different mix of nutrients results. Ideally, of course, no agrichemicals would enter the run-off and rivers, all would be absorbed into the crops, and contribute—and solely contribute—to giving high yields of healthy crops. Unfortunately, rain and plant growth are not that predictable, and to allow for errors, excess chemicals may be applied, and the surplus enters first the soil then the river or aquifer. Although in the 2010s great advances were made regarding chemical application, which is now a very precise science, and includes using satellite technology to apply the correct amounts of chemicals in the places that need them, and where such intensive management is possible. Other pollutions are further discussed below.

With all this variability, how can streams be classed on their nutrients? By using reference plant communities. For the more studious reader, and those particularly interested in statistics, Tables 1 and 2, shown at the end of this book, summarize this.

By using chemical analyses, the principal nutrients associated with a particular rock type and its plant distribution can be determined. Within the major divisions of rock type, the vegetation—both species assemblages and frequency—varies, partly due to the nutrient composition. Whether rock is resistant, limestones, or bog peat, the chemical composition differs. This is also partly due to the amount of silt produced. Most of the soil nutrients are in the silt (plus mud), and most of the river nutrients are in the soil rather than suspended in the water. And when the plants are analysed, it shows that there are usually far more nutrients in Chalkstream water than are in the plants. So there is something odd here. Vegetation strongly reflects the nutrient composition—but this is more than the plants need. Why? So far, no one knows. It may be a matter of balance between the major nutrients. This is undoubtedly important. Limestones have high calcium and lower other nutrients than other rock types whose total major nutrients are similar. But also there are all the minor and trace elements, and the organic substances (as described above)—a lot more research needs to be done…!

Downstream eutrophication

Something else not usually known, but at least more easily explicable, is downstream eutrophication. Another *"Do Not Know"*. Exactly what does each nutrient do at each concentration and balance? Even something as simple as why, for example, *Phalaris arundinacea* (Reed grass, Fig. 11a) can live under water in strongly limestone water but not in other types, and why non-limestone species do not grow as well there, are not known. Passing downstream from brook to small to large river, species assemblages change, and usually change from lower to higher nutrients. Sometimes the difference is small, sometimes it is large: up to from, say, semi-dystrophic (acid, low nutrient status) to semi-eutrophic (higher nutrient status). Even this, though, has complexities made up of three factors:

1. increased absolute change of nutrients in the sediments. This can occur without a change in habitat, but is great if there is a downstream loss of acid peat or acid woodland beside the river, by a change in the rock or subsoil type to a more fertile type (for example, Resistant rock upstream in the catchment changes to clay or alluvium downstream, by tributaries coming in from more fertile catchments, and by the addition of nutrients from activities such as farming and effluents)

2. increased sedimentation downstream when streams run off hills into lowlands and flatter ground, picking up sediment along the way

3. increased stream size and maybe a decreased flow type. This is apparent rather than real. Various nutrient-rich, water-supported species need space (depth) for good growth, so do not grow in small brooks. However, even if these are removed from the analyses, nutrient status bands still increase downstream.

What pollution does

Oddly, rather more is known about the effects of (some) pollutants on plants than the effect of the natural nutrients! The habitat chooses the plants to grow in it—from amongst those whose seeds or other propagules (fruit, bulb, rhizome, winter bud, stem fragment) are present. Those whose propagules do not develop are obviously not chosen by the habitat, and are excluded by (in this respect) the pollution present. They are also excluded by, for example, unsatisfactory nutrients, flow, depth, substrate, shade, management, disturbance and many more factors! So the first way pollution prevents good vegetation is by stopping germination, development or growth. When a species can live, but not grow well because of pollution, it is often over-small and probably unhealthy. Its weak shoots and roots can easily be killed (smothered by larger plants or species), eaten, or washed out. Plants become unhealthy if pollution is widespread, and effects differ in various ways, and in different species.

Every leaf has a bud in its axil (the angle where it joins the stem). To have good growth, a lot of buds must grow (Fig. 4), giving large, probably competitive, shoots—pollution hinders this. This hindering happens often, although proving it is another matter. There is a plausible but unproven idea that heavy metals act in this way, at least on *Potamogetons* (various

Fig. 4: Bud growth in the water

pondweeds). As with so many conclusions on plant behaviour, it is possible—but NOT proven. (Perhaps a full investigation should be carried out?) In one study, the heavy metal example did explain the peculiarity of toxic chemicals and good healthy *Potamogeton* shoots: that whilst they were indeed good and healthy, there were far too few of them and that pollution had prevented side shoots growing, rather than lessen their size or their looks.

Roots of water plants, like those of land plants, may be short, long, bushy or not (Fig. 5*).

Long roots particularly, and bushy ones secondarily, grip best in the soil—the substrate. So what? Rivers flow, flowing water dislodges plants, and takes loosely-rooted ones out of the ground. Standard town-pollution makes roots shorter and fewer and thus easier to wash out. There is good evidence of this.

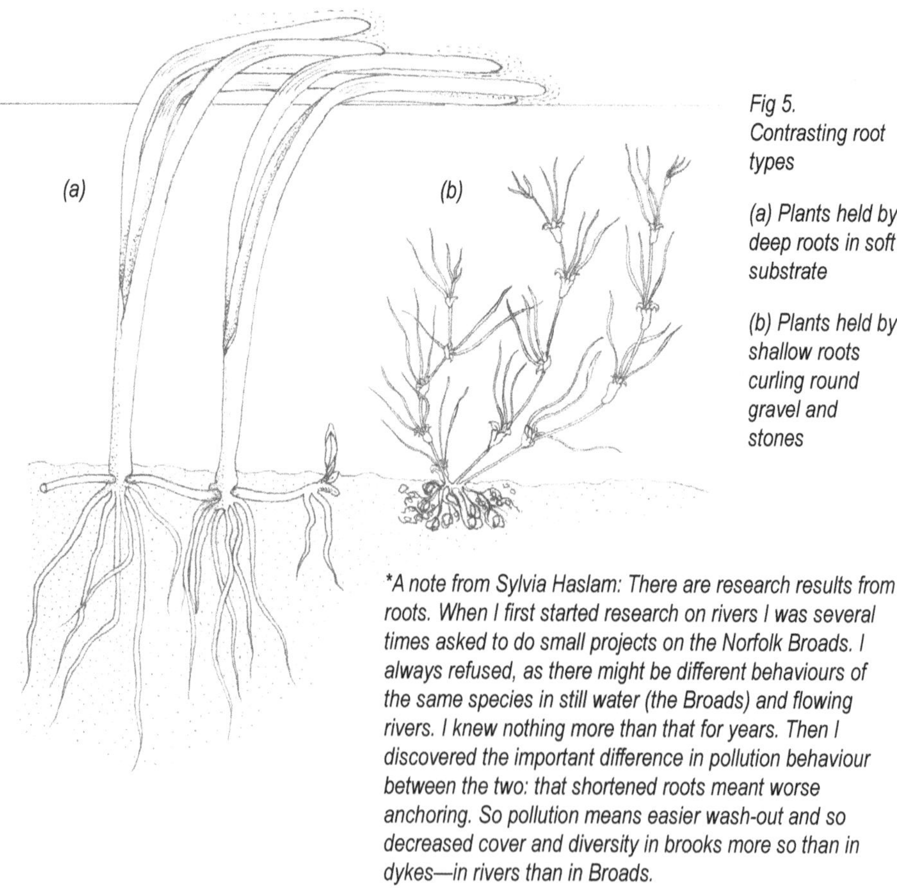

Fig 5.
Contrasting root types

(a) Plants held by deep roots in soft substrate

(b) Plants held by shallow roots curling round gravel and stones

*A note from Sylvia Haslam: There are research results from roots. When I first started research on rivers I was several times asked to do small projects on the Norfolk Broads. I always refused, as there might be different behaviours of the same species in still water (the Broads) and flowing rivers. I knew nothing more than that for years. Then I discovered the important difference in pollution behaviour between the two: that shortened roots meant worse anchoring. So pollution means easier wash-out and so decreased cover and diversity in brooks more so than in dykes—in rivers than in Broads.

Of course dykes and drains, which do not have wash-out flows, have plants behaving like those of lakes and ponds whose small root systems suffice to keep plants in place in ordinary weather. So in the same amount of pollution (which is virtually impossible to prepare or measure), the same species grow better in dykes, where they can stay and even form firm networks of roots; in streams, however, they are washed out and storms are too frequent for the plants to develop firm, stable root networks.

Incidentally, when pollution (or other damage) is enough to prevent some plant growth, the plants are increasingly restricted to the places they find "best", such as the most sheltered, the cleanest silt, or the deepest water. As habitats deteriorate, plants which could tolerate medium as well as least exposure are washed out (or are unable to develop, see above), and so the possible niches are decreased and the plants are fewer. This is obvious, but it has the interesting corollary that the recording method may influence the result! Which is not something usually considered. If a suitable niche occurs on average, say, every 10m, then recording from a point source will pick up perhaps 2–4 clumps of plants in the 25m range (or 30 clumps in 500m)—both of which are common recording lengths. Either way, the qualitative term for recording purposes is "occasional". However, a further decrease will lead to many 25m-reaches being without the species, whilst it will still be "occasional" if 500m or 1km stretches are recorded. So the shorter recording distance will pick up the increased damage, the longer one will not. And the general assessment of the river habitat may (or may not) reflect this. Yet another complication!

Figure 6 shows various types of river structure and vegetation; the different types are clearly distinct. Where damage is moderate (and this includes quite natural swift flows, enough to reduce vegetation), vegetation is distinctive, and easily recognizable. Diversity is often about 7–10 species in a length of 20–25m in a 4–8m wide stream (and correspondingly less or more in smaller or bigger rivers). In these rivers with very little to reduce species, niches abound and so do species, and richness can double. (Only there is a difference between an excellent habitat with lots of niches, and a double-habitat like chalk plus clay! Same result, different species, and different cause.) In fact only one river with such an excellent habitat has so far appeared in the literature: the Swedish Björka. Interestingly, it looks like any respectable lowland river: no cascades, large bars, or deep pools, just a good habitat. And a river illustrating, say, 18 species in 20–25m in contrast to, say, Fig. 1 7 with a bare river empty of vegetation.

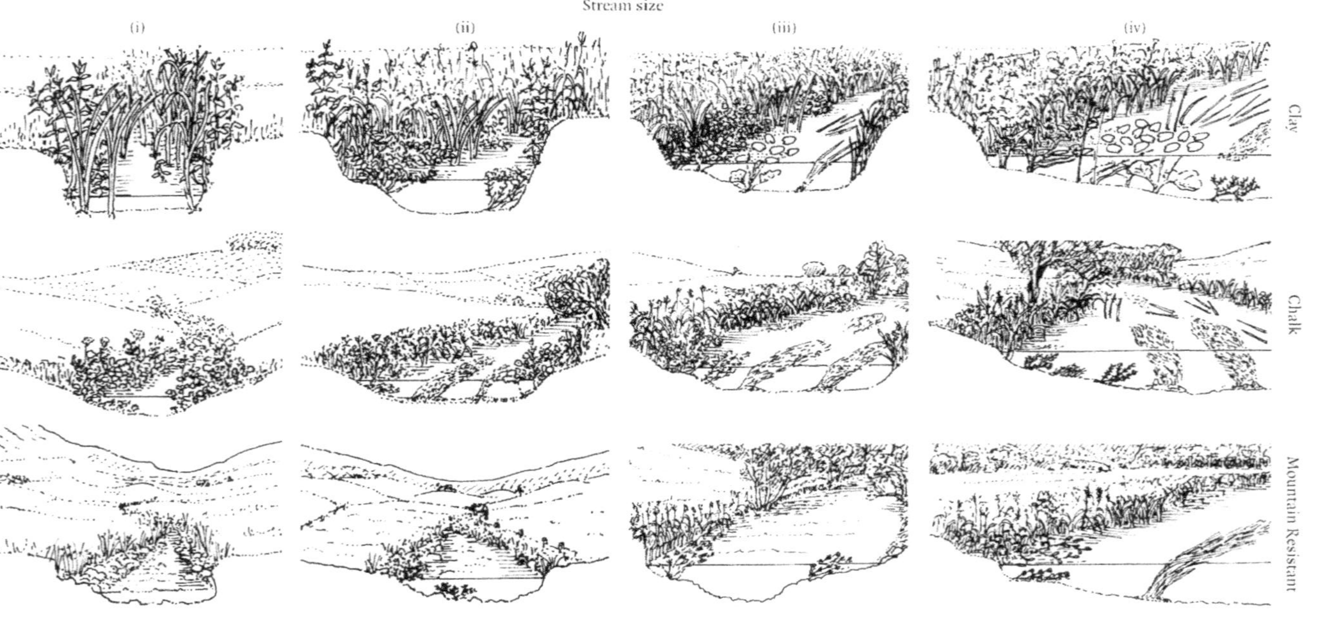

Fig. 6. River type in relation to stream size and rock type. Note the differences in channel outline, bank, water depth and flow, and in the vegetation type, diversity and coverage.

Stream Size Classification: Size (i) Small streams (brooks or ditches) without water-supported species (plants supported by the water, floating, and submerged species), up to 3m wide. Emergents (a plant mainly or entirely above water) can be present or absent. Size (ii) Small streams (brooks) with deeper water than (i) and with water-supported species, up to 3m wide. Water-supported species present, emergents present or absent. Size (iii) Medium streams (small rivers), 4–8m wide. Any type of vegetation (along the edges, or further into the water) or empty. Size (iv) Large streams (medium and large rivers), between 10–30m wide. Any type of vegetation or empty. (Illustration by Y Bower)

So much for the chemical influences of the natural materials, and the differences made by changing erosion, sedimentation and other disturbance. (Streams change position naturally—bends, meanders—so fresh substrate is constantly, however slowly, coming into the river. This is usually irrelevant for now.) On present knowledge, accumulation in silt and uptake by root hairs and thin-walled roots, and substrate changes by dumping and dredging, is like the processes for natural materials—more research wanted!

Substrates entering the water due to people are, of course, many, and variable in type, amount, concentration and effect, so here is but a brief summary. Anyone wanting to assess pollution by vegetation in a simple way—using a Government-approved method—should read *The River Scene: Ecology and Cultural Heritage* (Haslam 1997), available from Amazon, other leading bookshops, and Libraries.

Most common pollutants (those in most rivers, from domestic and town effluent):

1. hinder root development (their number, branching and size). Shoots can look healthy and full-size—or not. (Usually occurs closer to pollution entry than 2. or 3.)

2. produce reduced and unhealthy shoots, which are less branched (difficult to describe, but easy to recognise). Some species may become over-lush, instead (!)

3. cause discolouration of shoots, including yellowing of some edge species (particularly *Glyceria maxima* (Fig. 21b) and *Myosotis scorpioides* (Fig. 14c).

As anchoring lessens, plants are lost, so both diversity and cover decrease (easier wash-out).

However, different pollutants differ in their effect, and different species differ in their response to the same pollutant. What a surprise! And hardly anything is known for certain. Also, what a surprise!

Around the millennium the incidence of *Sparganium emersum* (strapweed, Fig. 26b), exploded. It became large and dense enough to shade out other aquatic plants. But, in site studies, emerged edge plants also vanished. These could not be shaded by *Sparganium emersum*. So why did they go? Again, research is needed.

When assessing pollution, there are two basic sides: one, the absolute levels of the pollutants; and two, their effect—the degree to which the vegetation differs to that of a clean river. For instance, in a river with a pool-and-riffle system and moderate pollution, more silt is dropped in the slow water of the pools. Therefore the pollutant concentration is higher. With the same conditions the pools have a more polluted flora. Looked at for basic nutrients, they are more nutrient-rich!

It is, in fact, easy to assess pollution by plants. All that is needed is diversity and cover data, plus a list of plants sensitive to and tolerant of the incident chemical influence, for example:

1. **Species most tolerant to town Sewage Treatment Works, Britain:**

(a) Most-tolerant—*Potamogeton crispus, P. pectinatus, Scirpus lacustris, Sparganium emersum, Sp. erectum, Enteromorpha* sp., blanket weed, (*Apium nodiflorum* small clay lowland *Mimulus guttatus* some small hilly)

(b) Semi-tolerant—*Agrostis stolonifera*, small *Glyceria* spp. (short leaves), *Butomus umbellatus, Glyceria maxima, Lemna minor* agg., *Nuphar lutea, Rorippa amphibia*, (*Phalaris arundinacea* hilly)

2. **Species most-tolerant to rice paddy pollution, Italy:**

(a) Near discharge, pollution severe—*Carex* sp.

(b) Downstream, moderate pollution—*Carex* sp., *Phragmites communis*

(c) Downstream, mild pollution—4 spp., e.g. *Carex* sp., *Phragmites australis, Callitriche* sp., *Ranunculus* sp.

(d) Downstream, near clean—6 or more spp., including *Callitriche* sp., *Ranunculus* sp.

3. **Species most tolerant to wash-house pollution, France**

(a) Near discharge, worst pollution (10m length)—Nil

(b) Downstream, improving—unhealthy *Callitriche* sp.

(c) Downstream, where small effluent enters—very unhealthy *Callitriche* sp.

(d) Downstream—healthy *Berula erecta, Callitriche* sp.

(e) Downstream and upstream, near clean—*Callitriche* sp., *Myosotis scorpioides, Phalaris arundinacea, Nasturtium officinale* agg.
Much: *Callitriche* sp.
Little: *Apium nodiflorum, Berula erecta*

4. **Two Sites downstream of Rugby sewage works (River Avon), showing recovery from pollution. All on lowland clay.**

(a) Stream size iii (4–8m wide), 4 spp., 80% cover
Much: *Potamogeton pectinatus*, Blanket weed
Little: *Callitriche* sp., *Sparganium erectum*

(b) Stream size iv (10–30m wide), 7 spp., 40% cover
Much: Blanket weed
Little: *Iris pseudacorus, Nuphar lutea, Potamogeton pectinatus,
Schoenoplectus lacustris, Sparganium emersum, Sp. erectum*

5. **Three Sites near the source of the River Witham, England, showing (over several years) recovery from pollution and damage from trampling. Lowland oolite. Stream size ii (4–8m wide and fairly deep).**

(a) No spp., badly polluted

(b) 3 spp., 20% cover
Little: *Rorippa nasturtium-aquaticum* agg., *Veronica beccabunga*, Blanket weed

(c) 6 spp., 50% cover
Little: *Lemna minor* agg., *Myosotis scorpioides, Rorippa nasturtium-aquaticum* agg., *Veronica beccabunga, Enteromorpha* sp., Blanket weed

This chemical measurement is, in principal, the same for any chemical influence that lessens roots and shoots of aquatic plants which lower diversity and cover.

The proportions of rock (and substrate) type can be assessed. So, for example, can town and domestic pollution, ochre, limestone, and blanket bog. (The active chemicals and their concentration are another matter!)

Water flow (like other natural features such as depth) also differentially affects different species. As for pollution, the reference vegetation is the optimum cover, diversity, and species type appropriate to the flow. At any point the reference vegetation can be worked out (and any other habitat be considered—faster, slower, more boulders). The actual vegetation can then be measured against the reference and the degree of, here, flow-damage assessed. Of course it is knowing how the character influences, which is important too!

An interesting thought. The minute amounts of substances smelt by animals ("My dog smelt yours 200m away!!") are considered fascinating. Tiny amounts of active pollutants in water, are considered dull. Why?

River Maps *(A different way of understanding rivers)*

The stylized river maps in this section are placed flowing from the top to the bottom of the figures. Where the mouths enter the sea, this is indicated by shading, and where they enter larger rivers, the rivers are named. Crosses (minor tributaries) are shown only if they have recorded sites. Rock type boundaries (small, solid line across river) are marked only where rivers are crossed. Landscape is indicated by the density of dots along the rivers.

Figures 7 and 8 form an interesting pair. These show river outlines with marked sites where the vegetation was surveyed. The dots show the landscape: the closer the dots, the steeper the land. Both these rivers are mainly lowland. The German River Neckar (Fig. 7) is without taller plants in all the sites recorded (apart from a tall monocotyledon, *Phalaris arundinacea*, in a tributary no bigger than a ditch).

This is vegetation as bad as any! None at all!

Now look at Figure 8, the Irish River Barrow (recorded *before* main river dredging). Plenty of

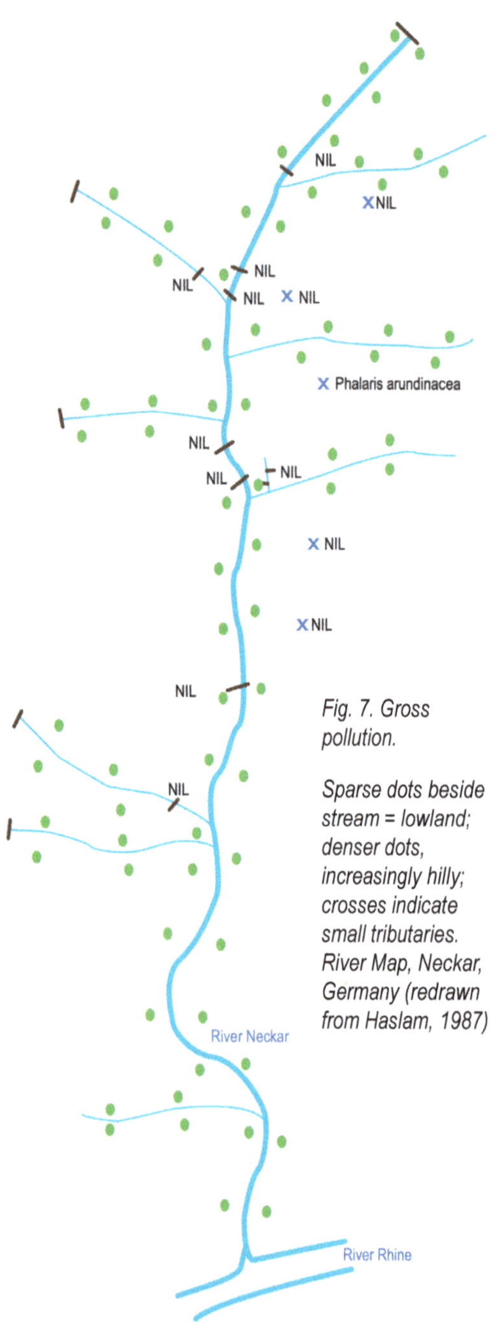

Fig. 7. Gross pollution.

Sparse dots beside stream = lowland; denser dots, increasingly hilly; crosses indicate small tributaries. River Map, Neckar, Germany (redrawn from Haslam, 1987)

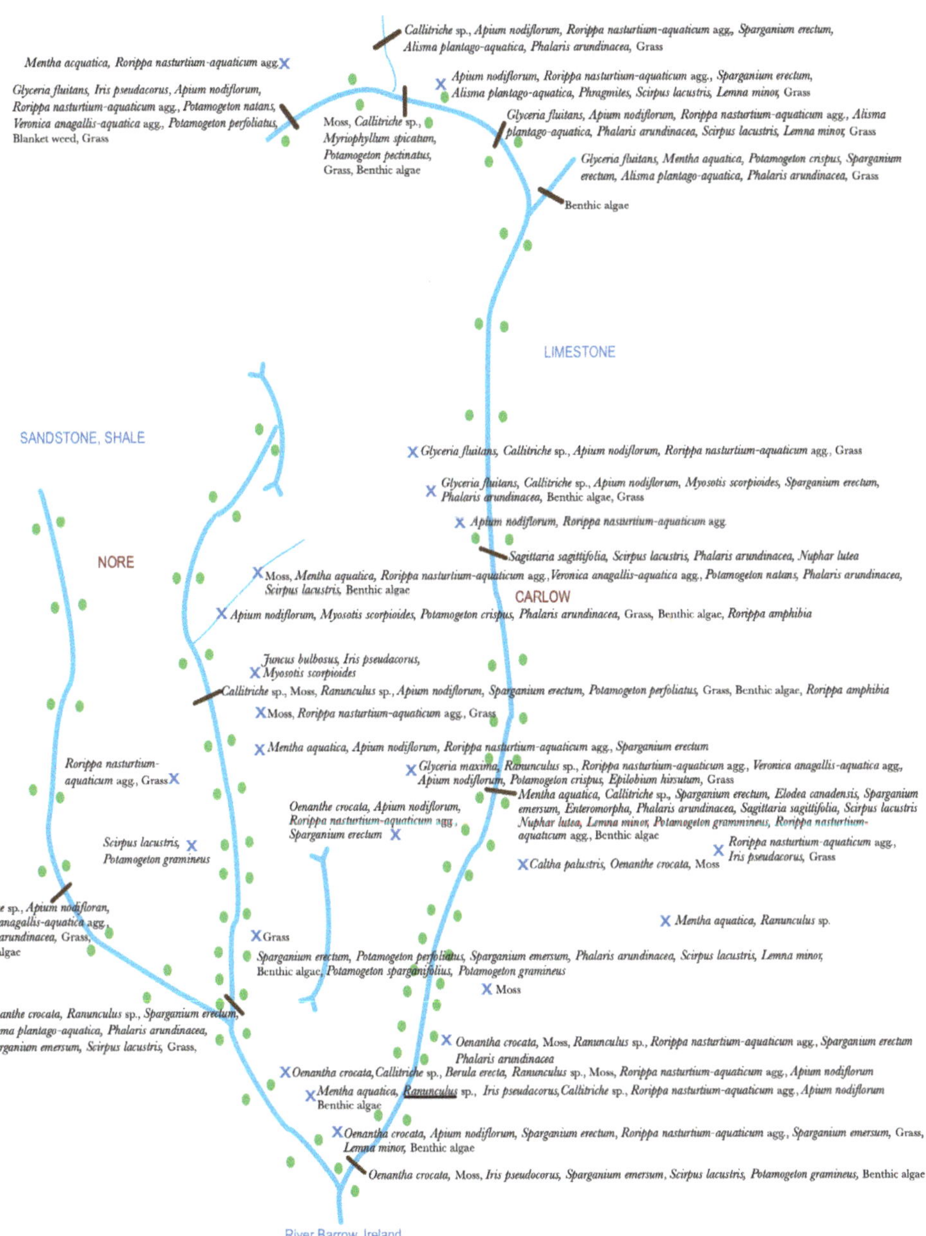

Fig. 8. River Map, Barrow. A satisfactorily good, clean river in Ireland (England has nothing as good). Only one species is abundant (underlined)—Ranunculus. There is a long species list per site, and the pollution-tolerant Blanket weed and Potamogeton pectinatus are rare

27

species! Not, of course, plenty at all sites: even the best-habitat rivers will have sites where vegetation is reduced by, for example, shade, cattle, waterfalls, shallows, bridges and other constructions, and recent maintenance operations.

But the River Barrow is amongst the "Very Good" in having so many of its recorded sites with a respectable high plant diversity.

This is comparing a very dirty lowland river (which should not be allowed in the 2020s) with a clean one.

But not all rivers with low vegetation have dirty water.

The French River Têt (Fig. 9) shows a very alpine river, too torrential for macrophytes (plants) except in locally sheltered places.

For less extreme British examples, there is the mountainous, Resistant rock River Vyrnwy in Wales (Fig. 10a), where swift spate-water keeps vegetation very low, and, in contrast, the River Itchen in Hampshire (Fig. 10b), on Chalk Downs, with good vegetation in reasonably clean limestone water. Later, much vegetation and species diversity was lost from this river, primarily because of water loss (abstraction) also because of increased pollution and disturbance. But Figure 10 shows that the present vegetation ought to be better, and that we, the people, have made it deteriorate.

The River Vyrnwy has not just fewer species, but different ones. Firstly, mosses are present at most sites. "Mosses" are a wide and ecologically variable group, but, being rootless, are helped and brought in by good firm stones to which they can adhere. If there is swift water like that of the River Têt in France, not even mosses can stick and grow. The absence of stones and rock in the stream bed make the habitat less suitable for mosses (hence in the lowlands the presence of mosses on bridges but not on easily-moved silt alongside—such moss records do not appear in the lists here unless specially marked). Overall there are more lower-nutrient than higher-nutrient mosses.

The River Vyrnwy has more mosses than the River Itchen for two reasons: the quality of the water and the flow of the water (flow is a controller for substrate texture). *Phalaris arundinacea* (Reedgrass, Fig. 11a) is the only other frequent species. So the plant community in the majority of—and excluding lower—River Vyrnwy sites is moss on rocks and Reedgrass on the edges. In addition, the small *Agrostis stolonifera* (Creeping bent grass, Fig. 11b) is

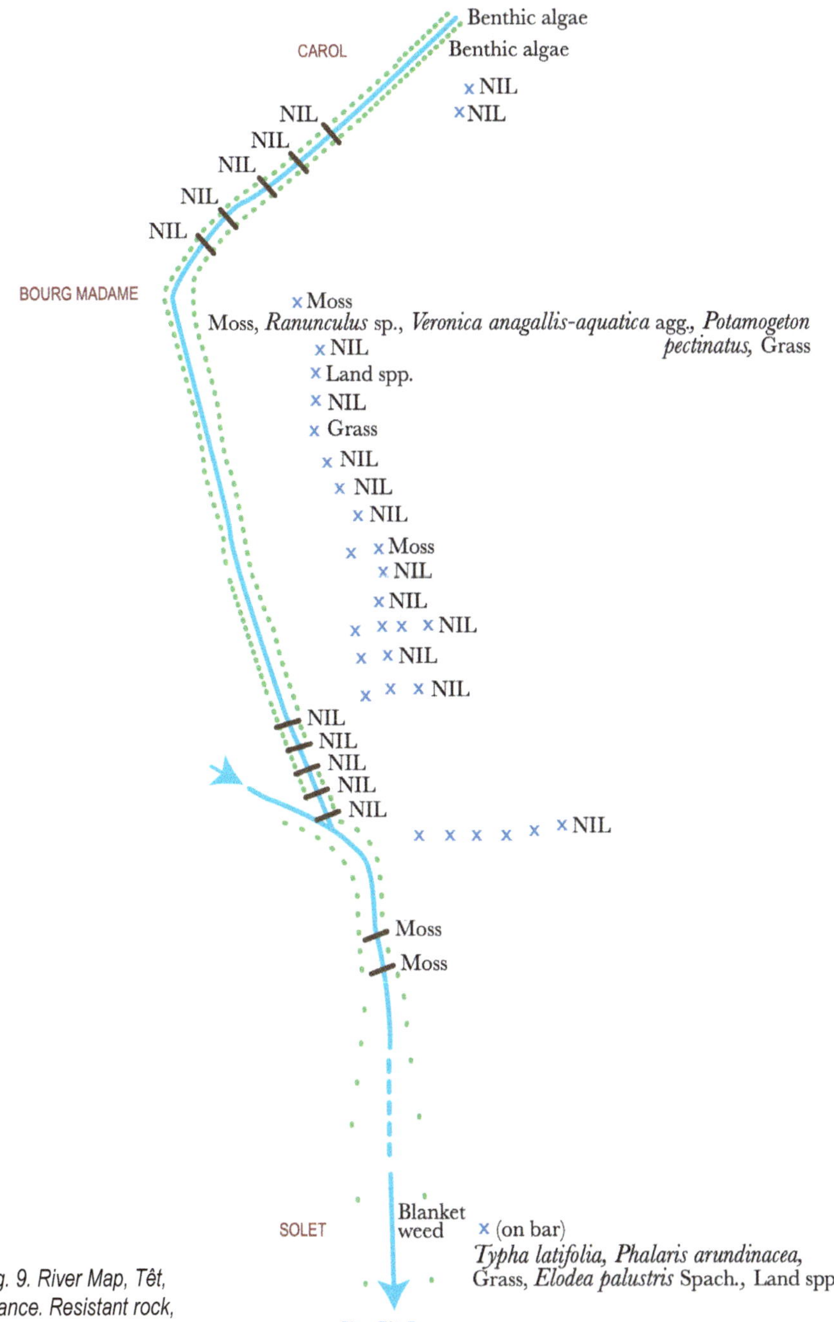

Fig. 9. River Map, Têt, France. Resistant rock, Alpine (1981)

29

Fig. 10a. River Map, Vyrnwy,
Britain. Resistant rock (mainly),
mountain (1973)
Key Fig 10a, b
N North
S South
E East
W West
C Central
SC Several Channels
u/s upstream
d/s downstream
Blanket weed
NIL
NIL
Moss, Grass
x Veronica beccabunga, Moss, Grass
Phalaris arundinacea, Moss, Benthic algae
Phalaris arundinacea, Moss
Phalaris arundinacea, Moss, Grass, Benthic algae
Veronica beccabunga, Benthic algae
Moss, Benthic algae
Moss, Grass, Benthic algae
Phalaris arundinacea, Moss, Benthic algae, Grass
Moss, Grass, Benthic algae
NIL
Phalaris arundinacea, Moss,
Grass, Benthic algae
Phalaris arundinacea x
Phalaris arundinacea, Polygonum amphibium,
Ranunculus sp., Callitriche, Moss
RESISTANT
Benthic
algae
Moss, Benthic algae
Phalaris arundinacea, Benthic algae
OSWESTRY
Moss, Benthic algae
Grass
Blanket
weed
Benthic algae
NIL
COAL MEASURES
ALLUVIUM SANDSTONE
Phalaris arundinacea, Ranunculus sp., Moss,
Sparganium erectum, Blanket weed, Other
Ranunculus sp.
Ranunculus sp.
River Vyrnwy
Phalaris arundinacea,
Ranunculus sp.
River Severn
N: Veronica beccabunga, Epilobium hirsutum, Other
S: Benthic algae
N: Ranunculus sp., Spaganium emersum,
Myriophyllum spicatum.
S: Benthic algae

Fig. 10b. River Map, Itchen, Britain. Chalk (mainly), lowland (1977)

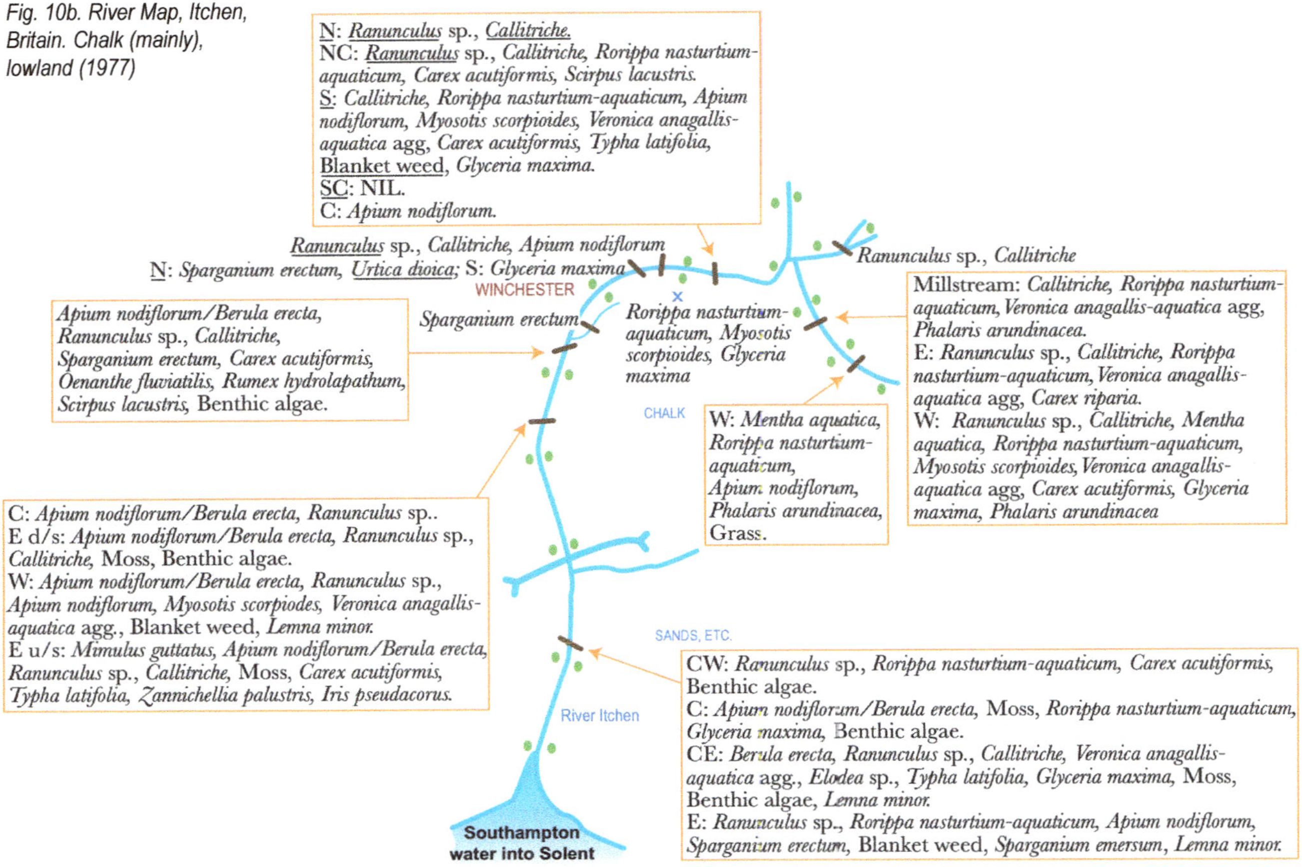

occasionally present, probably having been swept into the water by a storm flow (this grass can live for some time on fallen clods).

Another species, Blanket weed (Fig. 11c—trailing algae growing large enough to be easily seen), which forms a vegetation component, is present only just below a reservoir—where spates are restricted to when the sluice is opened, so the algae can grow between these. *Callitriche* spp. (Starwort. Fig. 11d) and *Veronica beccabunga* (Brooklime, Fig. 11e) occur enough to be listed as characteristic.

Further downstream, mostly where a nutrient-richer tributary has entered, there is *Ranunculus* (Water crowfoot Fig. 11f). Here the stream is also larger (more and deeper water) and with less swift (scouring) flow. There is one sizeable stream flowing in from a much more nutrient-rich rock—Coal Measures—which has increased species and cover.

The plant community of this part of the river can thus be recorded as:

> **Probable Species:** *Phalaris arundinacea*, mosses
> **May be associated:** *Callitriche* sp., *Veronica beccabunga*, *Ranunculus* sp..
> Number of species expected in 20–25m of this (reasonably undamaged) river: 2–3 (perhaps up to 5).
> **Cover of vegetation:** probably barely 10%.
> **Rare species found:** 0 (The "found" is important because the banks were walked only once, not the twice usually required—once in early and once in late summer.)

Fig. 11a. Phalaris arundinacea
(Reedgrass)

Fig. 11b. Agrostis
stolonifera
*(Creeping bent
grass)*

Fig. 11d. Callitriche *spp.*
(Starwort)

Fig. 11c. *Blanket weed growing over a weir and inset, growing amongst stones on the bed*

Fig. 11e. Veronica beccabunga
(Brooklime)

Such is true for the sites recorded and, if enough representative sites are seen, may be true overall. (May be? An inconspicuous rare plant will only be seen at a proper site stop.)

From just one river, and far-too-few species, we can therefore see a community—or the beginning of one. Vegetation is fairly consistent and depends on flow (landscape,

Fig. 11f. Ranunculus
(Water crowfoot)

substrate, texture, rock type), nutrient status (rock type, flow), and of course on human activities. It is when the data mounts up, giving species lists which are consistent, or else—like the record of Blanket weed in the River Vyrnwy—explicable as to why they are not consistent, that communities can be recognised.

Figure 12a shows part of the Aberdeen River Don and is a good example of what can happen. Here is a river system on Resistant rock, with various small streams, all potentially able to bear water-supported vegetation. The land is hilly but not mountainous, except where the main river originates. Vegetation is fair, of a hilly nature.

Look, though, at the Mossat stream (Fig. 12b)! There is far more vegetation—though size, landscape, flow, and so on, remain similar.

So? Rock type? Here is sandstone, a much more nutrient-rich rock type. Change of rock and soil type has changed the water and substrate nutrients in both absolute concentrations and in balance (ratios). The vegetation, in both diversity and cover, is strikingly better—all due (here) to the local outcrop of Old Red Sandstone. And that is due to the clean water of the quality developed on the sandstone. **Clean** water! But different chemically to that on Resistant

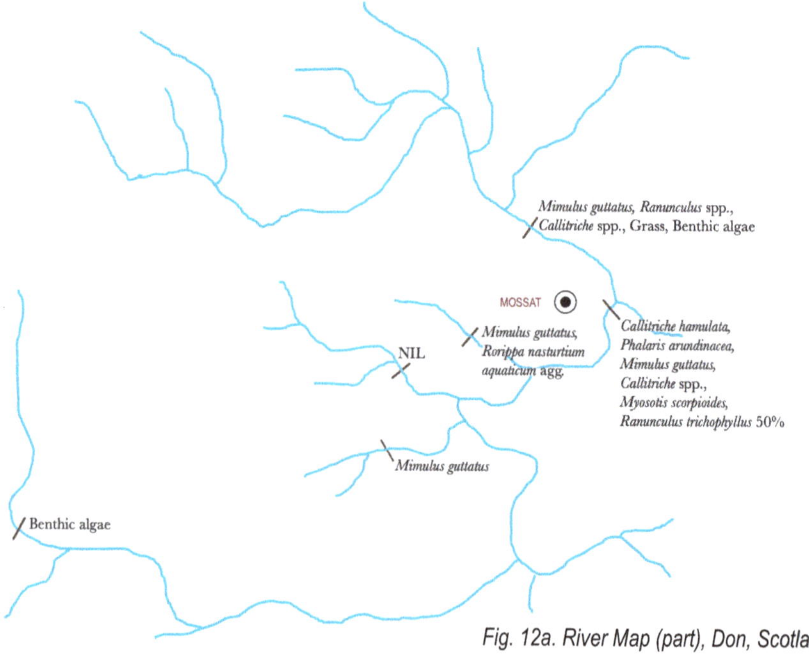

Fig. 12a. River Map (part), Don, Scotland

rock, therefore different in vegetation. (Note: although most plants take up more from the substrate than the water above, actual uptake in the substrate is from the associated water, not the substrate particles.)

It is interesting that the two sites are so different! Both have equal access (via birds, other animals, flow, and wind) to propagules of all species. Yet, with Resistant rock, water, diversity and cover are lower. Why? Unfortunately this question requires further investigation and is outside the remit of this small

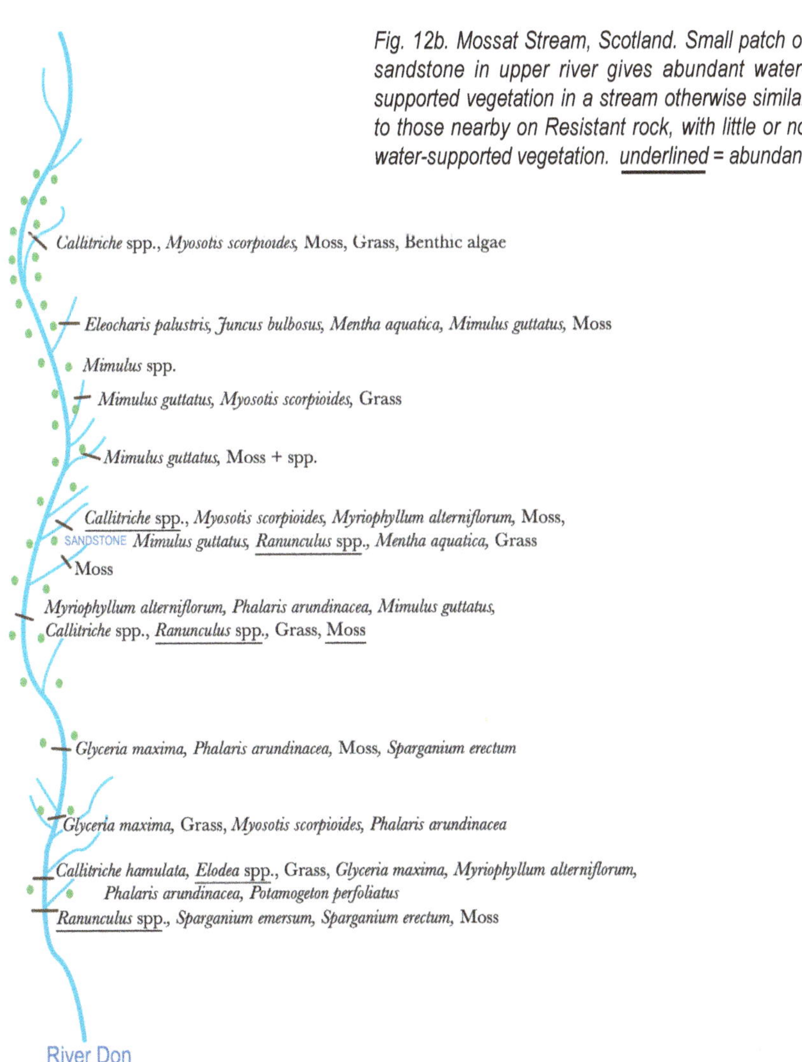

Fig. 12b. Mossat Stream, Scotland. Small patch of sandstone in upper river gives abundant water-supported vegetation in a stream otherwise similar to those nearby on Resistant rock, with little or no water-supported vegetation. underlined = abundant

book. However, preliminary observations indicated that the plants' roots were shorter, suggesting that Fringing herbs (the watercress-like group—short, wide-leaved bushy plants growing along stream edges) were more easily washed off, so anchoring less well on Resistant rock for the size of the plant.

A Case-in-Point

The River Itchen (Hampshire, Fig. 13 1–2) is very different to the River Vyrnwy in Wales (Fig. 13 3–4)—and not just because it is entirely in lowlands. That can account for the sparsity of mosses (too few large stones and rocks), but not for everything. (Note: *Apium nodiflorum* (Fool's watercress, Fig. 13 5) and *Berula erecta* (Water parsnip, Fig. 13 6) are easily separated when they have flowers above ground: *Berula* has tall umbels (clusters of flowers on several stalks, like the ribs of an umbrella) above the leaves, *Apium* does not, and the habit differs. But in the early growing season, the underwater leaves and those above water, are difficult to distinguish (Fig. 13 7–8). No flowers, same habit, and the two can mingle, so picking, say, three young *Berula* leaves in succession does not guarantee that the fourth will also be *Berula*.)

1–2. River Itchen, Hampshire (2011). Beautiful Chalkstream with many fringing herbs, Brown Trout, abundant long-leaved Ranunculus *(1), shorter leaved* Ranunculus, *and bright green* Callitriche *(2)*

3–4. River Vyrnwy, Wales. Boulders covered in mosses and no fringing herbs (3), and fast-flowing waters (4)

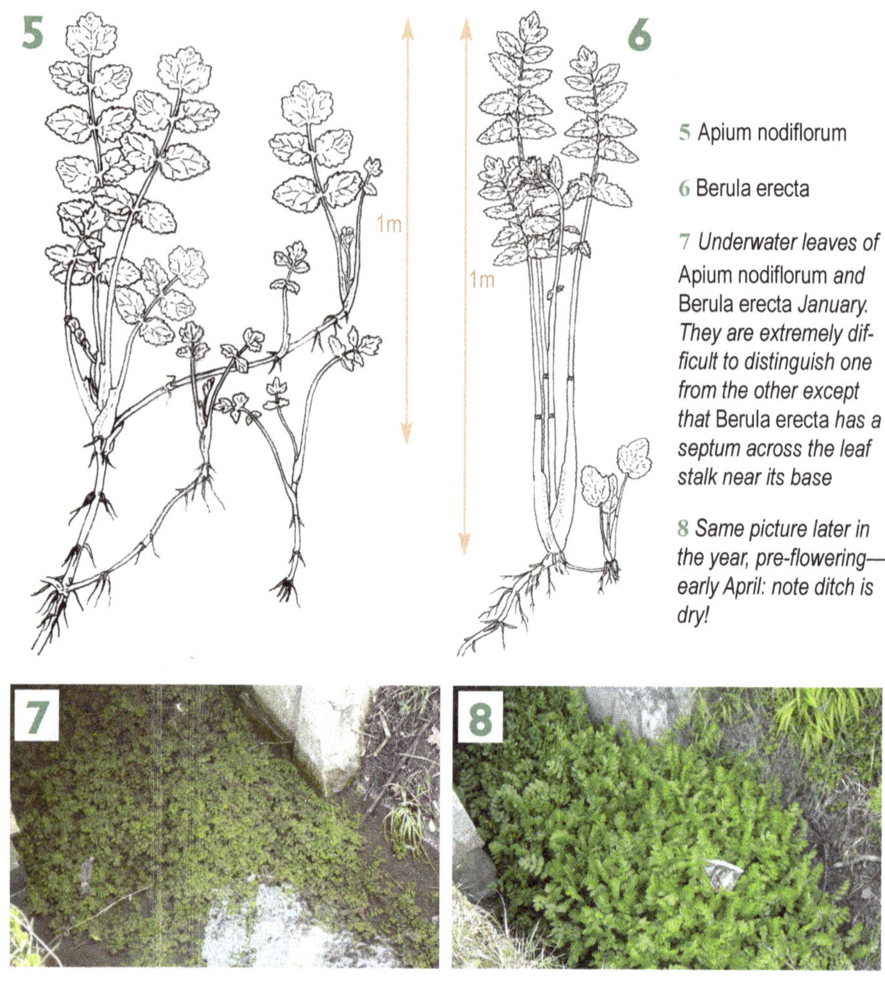

5 Apium nodiflorum

6 Berula erecta

7 *Underwater leaves of* Apium nodiflorum *and* Berula erecta *January. They are extremely difficult to distinguish one from the other except that* Berula erecta *has a septum across the leaf stalk near its base*

8 *Same picture later in the year, pre-flowering— early April: note ditch is dry!*

Several study sites on the River Itchen had nine species—nothing like River Vyrnwy! Six tall monocotyledons were recorded, not just one, and (as in Britain generally) *Sparganium erectum* (bur-reed Fig. 14a) was the most frequent (*Phalaris arundinacea*, Fig. 11a, would be more frequent in hill and mountainous rivers). Fringing herbs were not just represented by *Veronica beccabunga* (Brooklime, Fig. 11e, which indeed did not appear here) but by 6 others: *Apium nodiflorum*, *Berula erecta*, *Mentha aquatica* (Water mint, Fig. 14b), *Myosotis scorpioides* (Water forget-me-not Fig. 14c), *Rorippa nasturtium aquaticum* (Water cress Fig. 14d) and *Veronica anagallis-aquatica* agg. (Water speedwell Fig. 14e). There were a full dozen water-supported species: very respectable. None, though, would properly qualify as rare species at the time, though *Oenanthe fluviatilis* (River water-dropwort Fig. 14f) almost does now (2020). This species, common in the 1930s, was more localized in the 1970s, occurring mainly in limestone/clay mixed catchments. What is odd is the absence (in the recorded sites) of *Potamogeton* spp., once so common. This is an unsolved mystery, though Danes and Germans may well be right to attribute it to machine management.

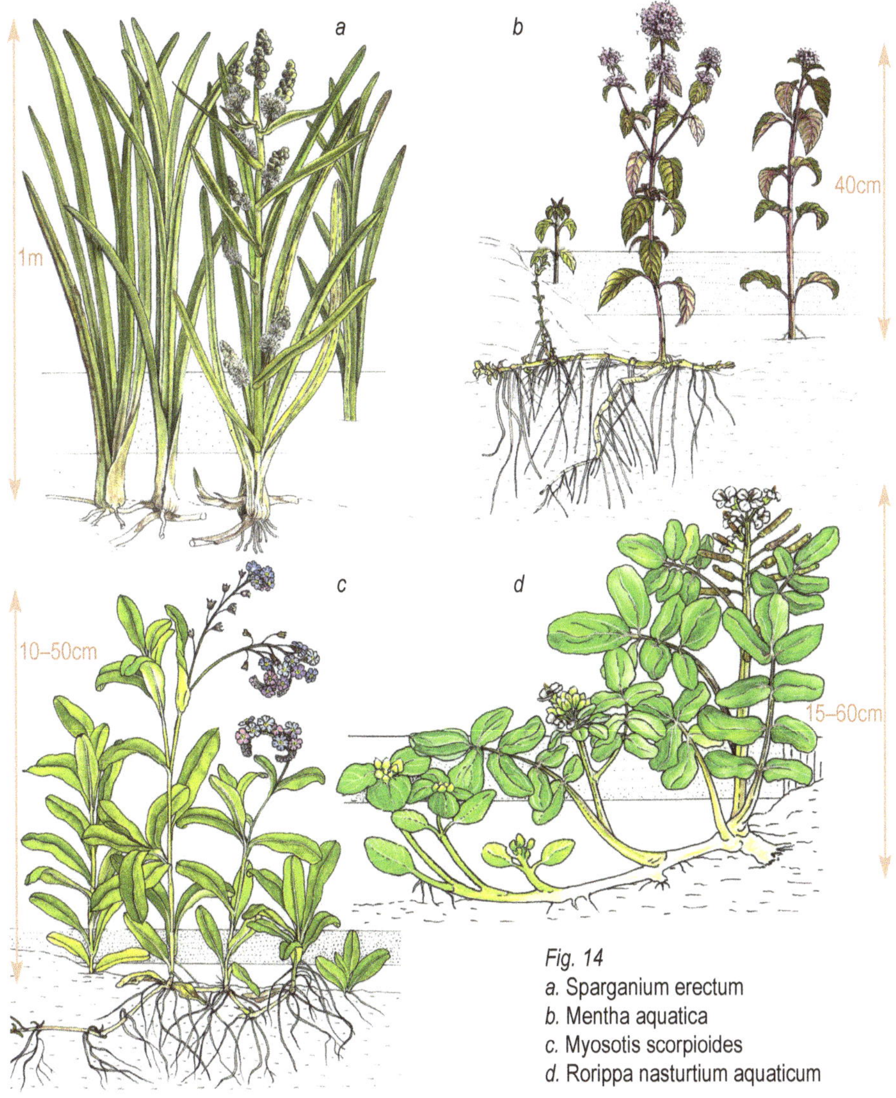

Fig. 14
a. Sparganium erectum
b. Mentha aquatica
c. Myosotis scorpioides
d. Rorippa nasturtium aquaticum

Fig. 14e. Veronica anagallis-aquatica *agg.*

Fig. 14f. Oenanthe fluviatilis

Fig. 15. Elodea canadensis

The River Itchen is one of those southern Chalkstreams with superb trout fishing and highly experienced river-keepers to ensure trout populations thrive (which, with present-day abstraction, water loss from aquifer and land, pollution from development and population, and the ministrations of authorities, they probably cannot maintain at a high level). If keepers disapproved of a species, out it came. The nineteenth century import of *Elodea canadensis* (Canadian pondweed Fig. 15) could be worded as "That Evil Weed", fully accounting for its absence in much-managed Chalkstreams.

Small and disturbed channels have few species. Looking at the whole river, however, clearly 8+ species are to be expected at each recorded site. *Ranunculus*, *Callitriche* and Fringing herbs form the basic community, with a wide (compared with the River Vyrnwy!) variety of other species often or perhaps present. But rare ones are on the list. How come—when flow has been removed from the analysis?

The answer is in the number of niches, or varieties of habitat diversity. What does such a river look like, supposing the vegetation was removed and all else left untouched? First, obviously, a stream has banks on both sides and a bed in the middle. There are many habitat variations here, where plants with different preferences can find suitable habitats: different substrates, flows, depths, nutrients, shelters, potential grazing and other disturbance (Fig. 16a–h).

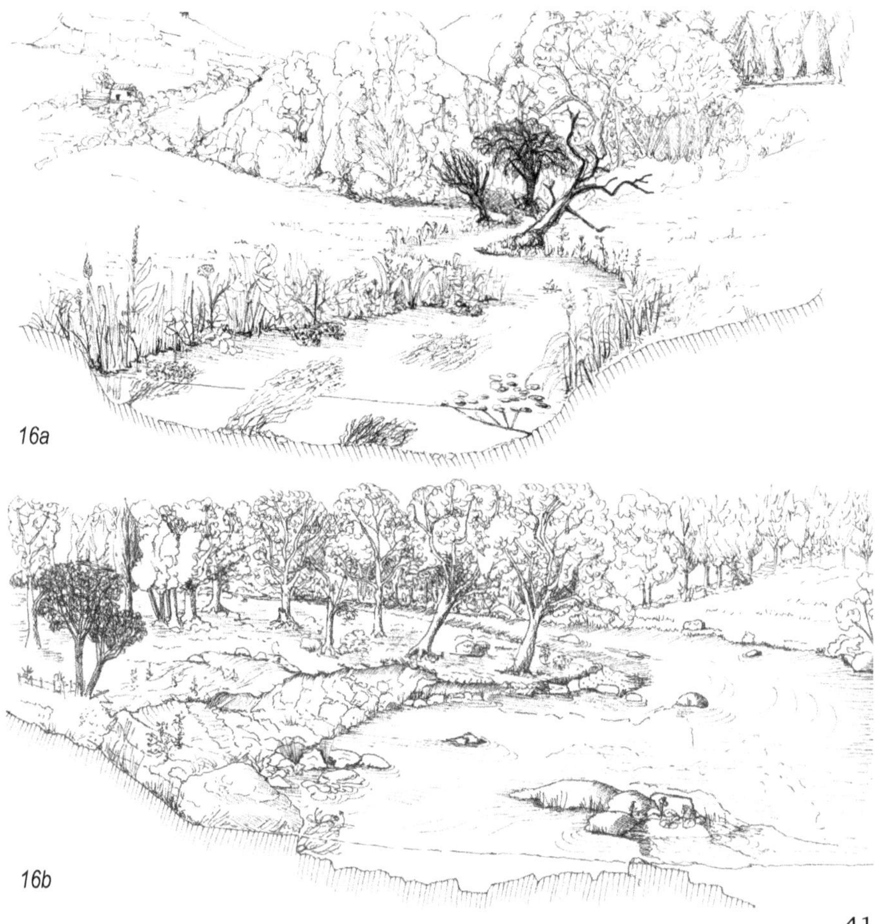

16a

16b

16c

Fig. 16a–c. Rivers should have much diversity in their architecture. Architecture is composed of physical structure and vegetation, and either or neither may be the more important

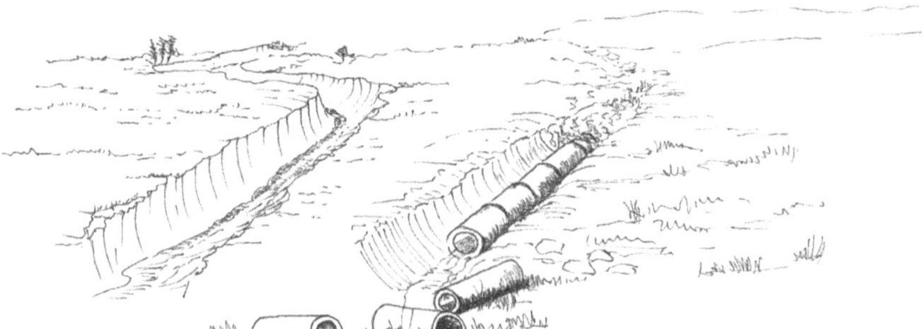

16d

16e

16f

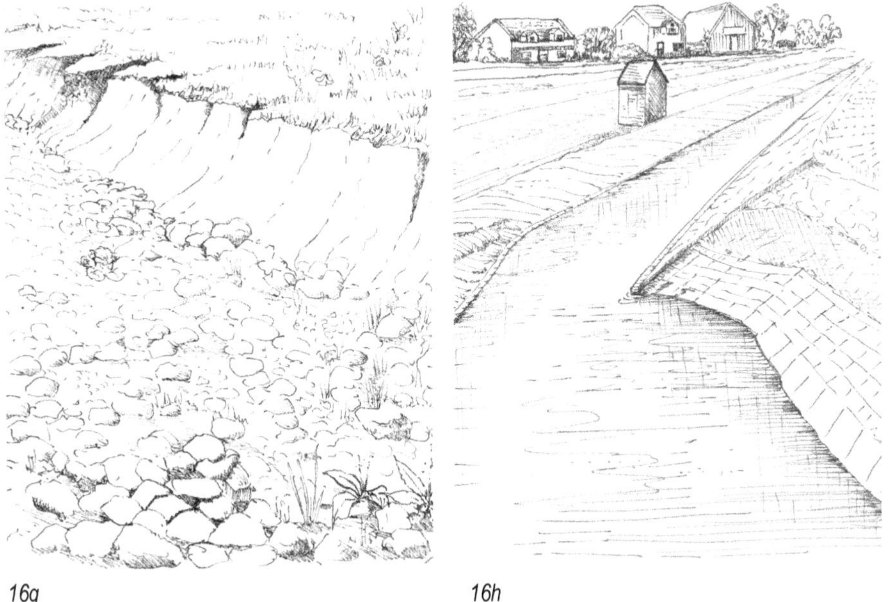

16g   16h

Fig. 16d–h. Rivers should not be over-disturbed, over-channelled, over-dried, over-drained or over-dredged

Ecology, of course, is never that simple! Whilst the above paragraph is true, it is not the whole truth. Niche variation means plant variation and therefore pollution variation.

Previous studies have shown some of the highest European species-richness areas to be the Giara Plateau in south-central Sardinia (Fig. 17), parts of Ireland, and Galloway in south-west Scotland. In all these places there was abundant structural (architectural) diversity fully illustrating this. Regrettably, since that research was carried out in the 1970s, the species-richness in the Irish and Scottish areas has declined, mainly due to drainage, which has also affected banks and substrate. And loss of water alters water regime, so again changes pollution.

Fig. 17. Wild horses graze on the Giara Plateau where there is still an abundance of flora, e.g., pink Sea Bindweed, Calystegia soldanella, the golden yellow Whorlflower, Morisia monanthos, and Ranunculus (white flowers abundant in the water, central background), which thrives in the marshes and shallow summer pools

Substrate (soil)

Erosion tends to be greatest in winter when the soil is less protected, as much vegetation has died back, and storm flows are more frequent and have greater discharges. Some species have more seasonal variation in plant structures than others, and therefore more differences in seasonal erosion as shown, for

44

example, in Figure 18a–c. Plants susceptible to erosion often have small root systems, so that only a little soil need be disturbed before the whole plant is loose. Similarly, larger plants of any species are usually more tolerant than smaller ones, as their root systems are larger. Rhizomatous species are less easily eroded if a rhizome network is present than if shoots are isolated. If other factors are equal, plants able to grow on several substrate types (for example,

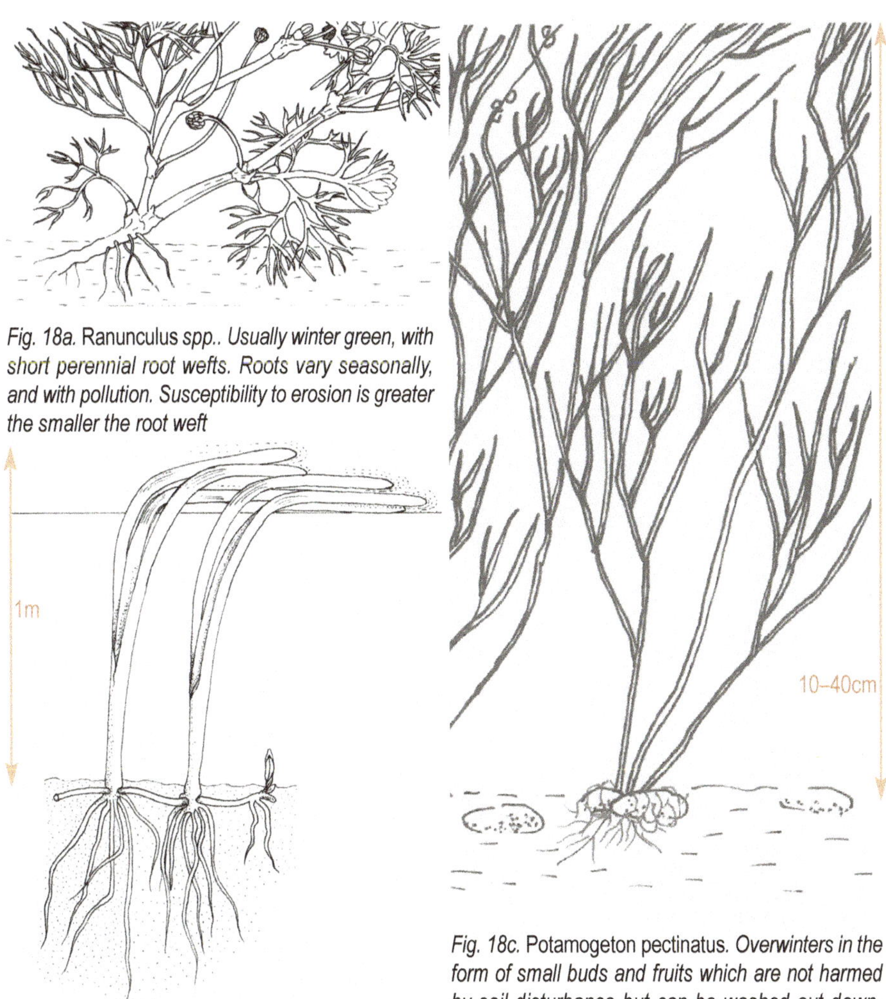

Fig. 18a. Ranunculus *spp.. Usually winter green, with short perennial root wefts. Roots vary seasonally, and with pollution. Susceptibility to erosion is greater the smaller the root weft*

Fig. 18b. Sparganium emersum. *Summer-green with deep roots, winter die-back, and slow death of roots in winter. Particularly susceptible to erosion in late winter*

Fig. 18c. Potamogeton pectinatus. *Overwinters in the form of small buds and fruits which are not harmed by soil disturbance but can be washed out downstream. Small plants are vulnerable to wash-out in spring, and in particular are weakened by pollution. In summer the rhizome system is deep and complex, and difficult to remove, though easy to damage*

Callitriche spp., *Rorippa* spp.) are usually eroded more easily on fine soil, as this is moved by slower water flows than are coarser particles.

Differential effects of erosion are demonstrated well by the Great Willowherb (*Epilobium hirsutum*), a pink-flowered common plant of stream banks frequently found in channels of narrow lowland brooks with little erosion. It has annual stolons about 20cm long. When these are even partly held in the compact soil of the bank they are almost immovable, even if the soil around them is lost. However, shoots of the second year's growth, away from the bank, are likely to have no connection with the bank, and are easily eroded, particularly in spring before the roots are full-grown (Fig. 19) These bushy shoots have a high hydraulic resistance to flow, and of course this increases losses. Eroded shoots may become established further downstream, but though shoots grow well under water the stolon (creeping stem) fragments necessarily lie on the soil, above the ground. This makes the plants extremely vulnerable, combining a high resistance to flow, easy erosion and low anchoring strength. Most plants are washed away before mid-summer. In the same way some fringing herbs are stable in ordinary storms if anchored in the bank, but are also easily washed off if they grow away from the bank.

Fig. 19. (a) Epilobium hirsutum *showing stable plant in the bank, and growing in the water before being washed away*

(b) The pink flowers of Great Willowherb (Epilobium hirsutum)

A part-pollution difference which affects animals more than plants is the soil surface. A nice trickle of moving, shallow water prevents silt accumulating on a gravel or stone base, and this provides a particularly good habitat for many invertebrates and, for example, trout eggs. In slower flows, a silt layer is likely to develop on the slow-moving bottom, with a quite different invertebrate (and vertebrate) fauna.

Soil is consolidated by root wefts and dense rhizome networks and so erosion is made difficult. *Zannichellia palustris* (Horned pondweed, Fig. 20a) is unusually erosion-tolerant for a short-rooted plant in fine soil, since its root weft is extremely intricate. However, if the weft is broken, erosion can be very quick. This could be caused by accident, for example animal trampling, or by pollution (softening substrate). Even in a soft substrate, the close rhizome network of *Schoenoplectus lacustris* (Common club-rush, Fig. 20b) is important in preventing large losses.

The very erosion-tolerant species form two groups: those which have rooted and rhizome wefts firmly entangled in coarse consolidated substrates (though these plants are susceptible to erosion when they happen to occur in unconsolidated soils); and those that have large networks of rhizomes and deep roots. *Nuphar lutea* (Yellow water lily, Fig. 21a) is an example of the latter. It has deep rhizomes which are sometimes eroded in storms, and these are so large that their high hydraulic resistance to flow means that they are easily washed downstream. *Glyceria maxima* (Reed sweet-grass, Fig. 21b), another of this group, has shallow rhizomes, so that parts losing contact with a firm anchorage point are vulnerable. Erosion is greatest for species growing in unconsolidated fine soils and is minimized when the plant has deep roots, a root weft, or if plants are attached to the bank—in which case pollution has less effect. An interesting difference occurs between brooks and dykes; the latter having little flow or scouring so that their fine soil is hardly moved and can be consolidated by roots (Fig. 21c). Once it is consolidated, erosion is difficult. Unconsolidated sand of course erodes rather more slowly than unconsolidated silt. Consolidated sand or stone is firm. When there is a hard bed with loose sediment above, rhizomes in the silt above, for example of *Sparganium erectum*, are more easily eroded than those in the hard bed such as rhizomes of *Schoenoplectus lacustris*. A hard bed of clay is eroded more easily than a bed of gravel.

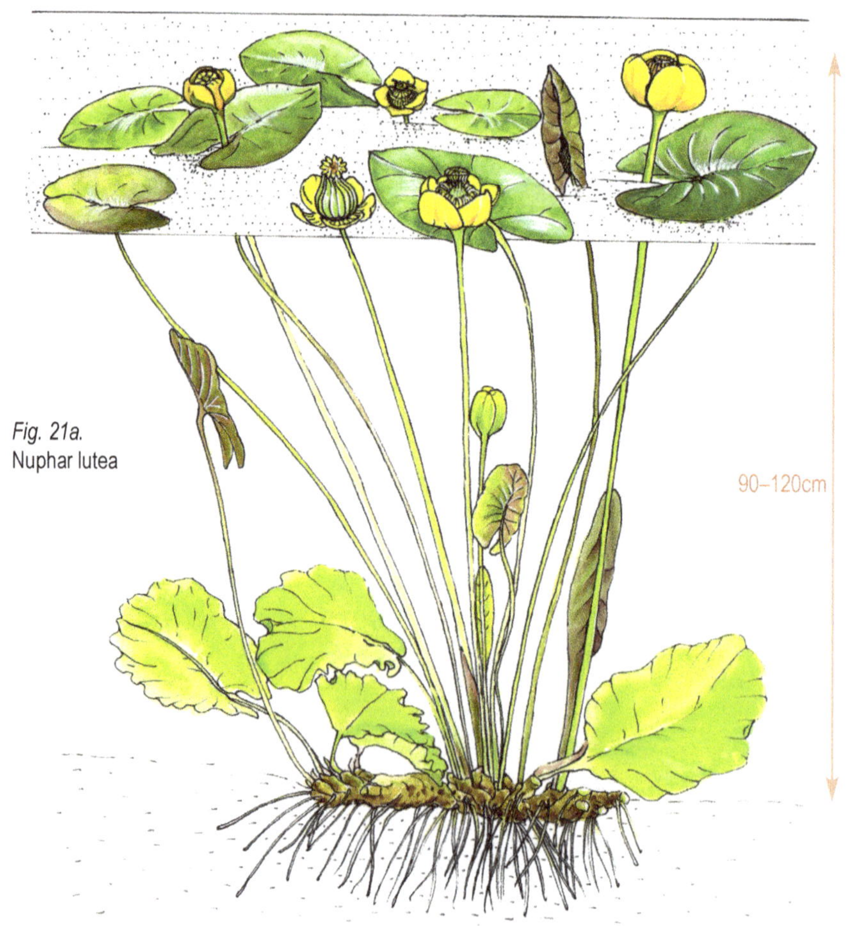

Fig. 21a.
Nuphar lutea

Fig. 21b. Glyceria maxima

Fig. 21c (below).
Brook and dyke
sections

(i) A brook: uncon-
solidated sediment
at the sides

(ii) A dyke: sediment
consolidated by the
roots of living and
dead plants

1m

(i)

(ii)

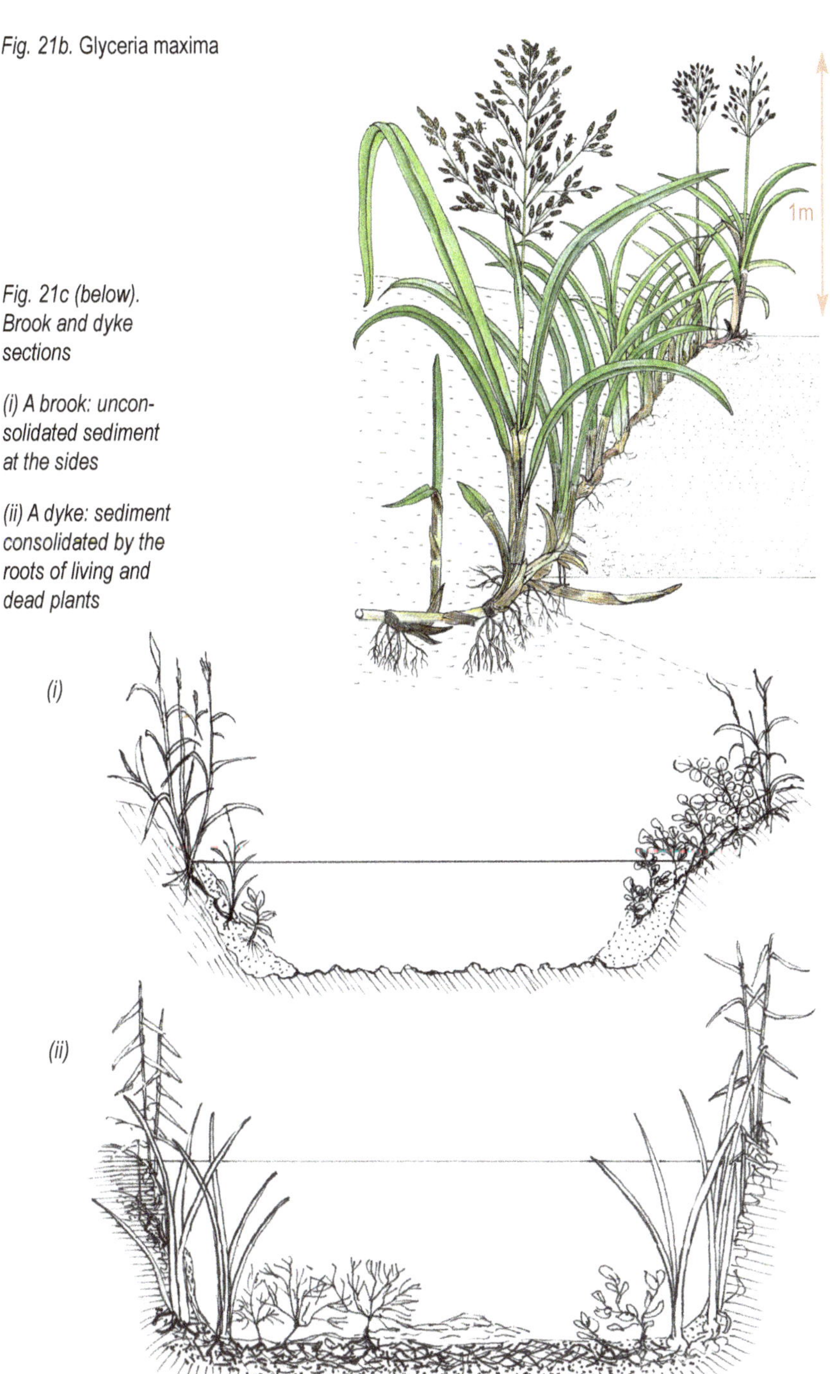

Vegetation pattern may be closely correlated with soil stability, as demonstrated in Figure 22 which shows substrate variation may create a secure haven and have an effect on plant damage before (a) and after (b) a storm. Figure 22 (c) shows a medium-size, hard rock stream in the Southern Apennines (Italy) with unstable, unconsolidated stone and gravel bed. Banks are over-uniform but okay. The left side has loose stone; the right side, shading by trees. The bed is quite nice to look at, but is really bad for river life. Water plant species are totally absent.

Fig. 22(a)

Fig. 22(b)

Fig. 22(c)

Research site example:
Temple Bridge (TL 7585 7287), River Lark, Suffolk, Fig 23

At the Old Bridge (ford, Fig. 23 2) there were the remains of a consolidated hard bed. *Ranunculus fluitans* (the long-leaved one) grew well. By 2020 most of the hard bed had disappeared. Shoots grew out on to the softer soils around, but if growth was poor with small shoots, the plants were washed off in a storm. Larger plants developed root wefts, which consolidated the soil somewhat and made erosion less easy, yet *Ranunculus fluitans* was effectively confined to the firm gravel at this site, because only there was it resistant to erosion. The firm gravel was the remains of the hard bed. (When rivers are dredged the upper substrate is removed. This may have been untouched for centuries, and become firm. Or may have been dredged only a few years ago and/or still be soft.)

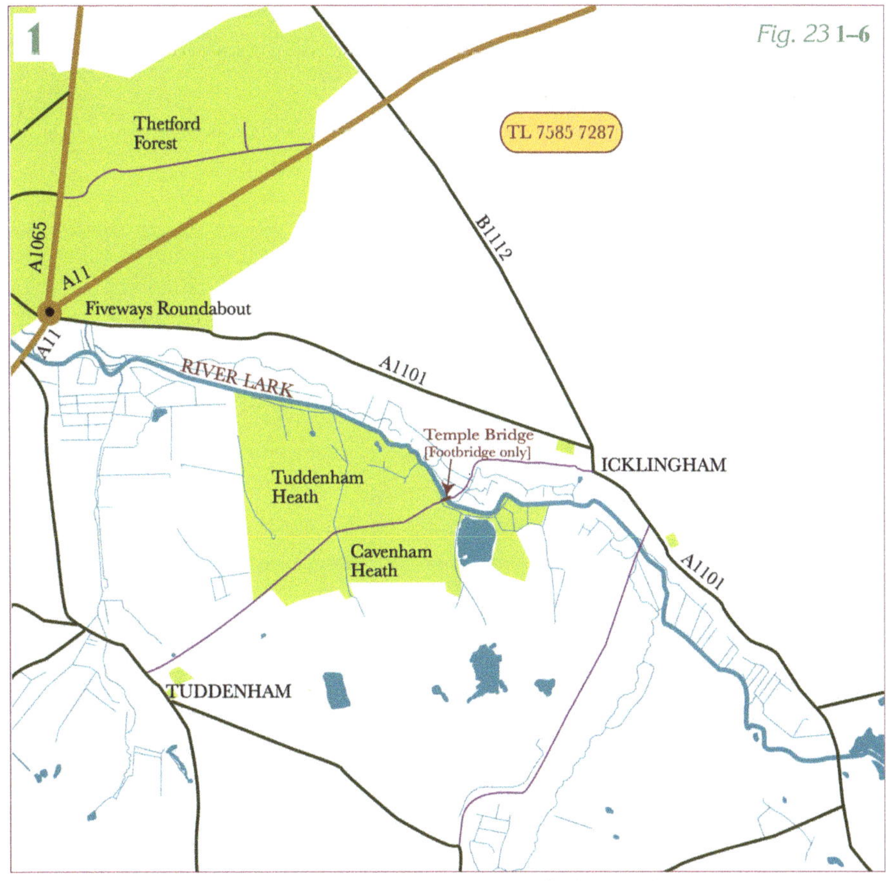

Temple Bridge. Map shows its location on the River Lark, now a footbridge only

Temple Bridge before it was demolished (c. 2002), showing much deterioration

2013: Remnants of Temple Bridge foundations

2012: "New" ford crossing by foot or bike, just downstream of Bridge remains. No Ranunculus

Alien Signal Crayfish (Pacifastacus leniusculus) are abundant amongst the rubble of the Bridge which remains on the bed of the river. These two young "entrepreneurs" were catching them by the bucketful to sell to a local restaurateur (2011)!

New footbridge, downstream of the original road Bridge, built in 2012 with new weir. Built on site of old stanch. A stanch divided the river into two. One side had a weir which could hold up water and be moved up and down (a simple lock, that is) so that barges and other boats had passage; the other side had free-flowing water. The river took much traffic, particularly up to the former abbey town of Bury St Edmunds

That which is unseen can also affect diversity. At Temple Bridge, which in the 1970s had a reasonable diversity, species grew according to the condition of the substrate.

Figure 24 is a schematic diagram showing *Potamogeton pectinatus* (Fennel pondweed) dominating in deep silt and slow flow (a), its density downstream dependent on flow in terms of how many winter buds or fruits are washed down. In spring, young plants are fairly dense on the softer soils, but these are easily eroded, and if storms in May are severe hardly any plants survive; whilst if storms are absent *Potamogeton pectinatus* can be nearly co-dominant. The softer mixed substrates (b) bear *Sagittaria sagittifolia* (Arrowhead) and *Sparganium emersum*, with sufficient stones present to protect the plants from erosion.

Unlike *Potamogeton pectinatus*, these two species have rhizomes living through the winter, so some of the plants occur in havens.

The mosaic of mixed-grained substrates (c) bear *Sparganium emersum* and *Potamogeton pectinatus* on the softer patches. These have straight roots which anchor by growing deep. On the firmer patches *Oenanthe fluviatilis* (River water-dropwort) and *Potamogeton crispus* (Curly pondweed) can grow. These have curly root wefts which anchor in gravel. The firmest substrate is hard gravel (d), where *Ranunculus fluitans* (River water-crowfoot) is dominant.

When moving water carried suspended particles these were deposited when the flow was checked for any reason, such as the land becoming flatter or plants forming obstructions. There were two basic responses to this. Either the plants

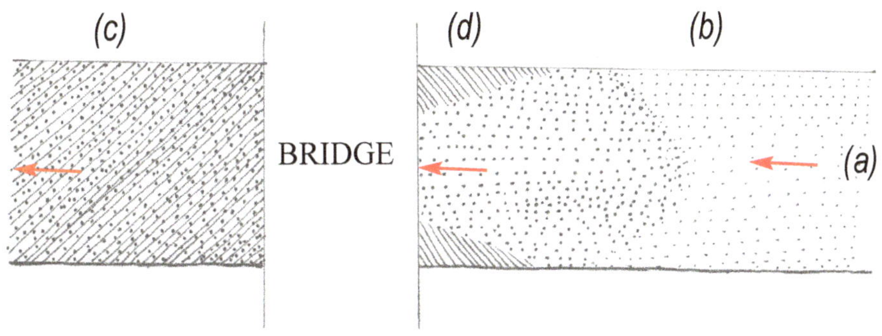

Fig. 24

kept their rooting level on the hard bed, whilst the sediment built up above, or they varied their rooting level so that it remained at ground level, even though this ground level was changing (Fig. 25).

All species varied somewhat between these two alternatives (although individual plants can show just one extreme). Once upon a time there presumably was a hard bed all over, but by the time of the research it was local (near the bridge: main dredging usually removes hard beds). On it, *Ranunculus* with its mesh of high-level short roots could anchor and grew well in the gravel.

So far, so good. Wonderful plant diversity associated with substrate type. But with a single type of water, substrate type may still vary chemically. Silt is the most nutrient-rich. Sands are comparatively nutrient-poor because they hold so little silt. Gravel is often likewise, but in slow flow silt can be held between or above the particles. Stones move less, so often appear more nutrient-rich if the silt stabilizes between the stones. So nutrient status depends on the substrate— chemically as well as physically.

Going back to the earliest records from the 1920s (R.W. Butcher), *Potamogetons* and total diversity are less, perhaps due to the regular annual cutting being by machine, not manually. In the 1950s, *Ranunculus* was abundant: a white sheet of flowers, in May. The hardbed was presumably disappearing, leading to the loss of *Ranunculus* but the substrate below was showing and variable. At the start of research, with what would now be excellent, mainly chalky, vegetation, there was concern about pollution from a sugarbeet factory. Would all rivers be like this! In the 1950s the white (in May) band was still there. Drainage of the valley, and its springs, was—though unrecognised at the time—becoming serious, so the incoming clean water would have been less. River depth was presumably less, at least in parts.

So, the early records show a chalk (other, including sand) vegetation, with much variation due to the substrate and its chemistry. Then two changes in water quality occurred which overrode the then patterning and substituted a luxuriant vegetation of species which were tolerant to these pollutions. From a mosaic to monodominance, and then signs of a mosaic again.

So far, so good—or so bad! Although anyone working on river vegetation for a few years often thinks it is stable—this is often not the case. Here, as the millennium (2000) approached, pollution worsened and the *Potamogeton pectinatus* not only grew larger, but by virtue of getting larger, smothered and shaded the other species and dominated. Not long-term though. By 2010 the pollution was still bad but had changed in its chemical nature and the vegetation was overtaken by larger, really vigorous *Sparganium emersum* (Fig. 26), as happened over so much of England at that time. In a few years, it, too, was retreating, and other species were starting to return, including fringing ones: lost during the bad pollution.

Both these major changes were in the water—clear water, but not clean water, getting into the silt, so dirtying the substrate and changing all the chemical status.

How complicated! But also how logical and how fascinating—like so much about river plants.

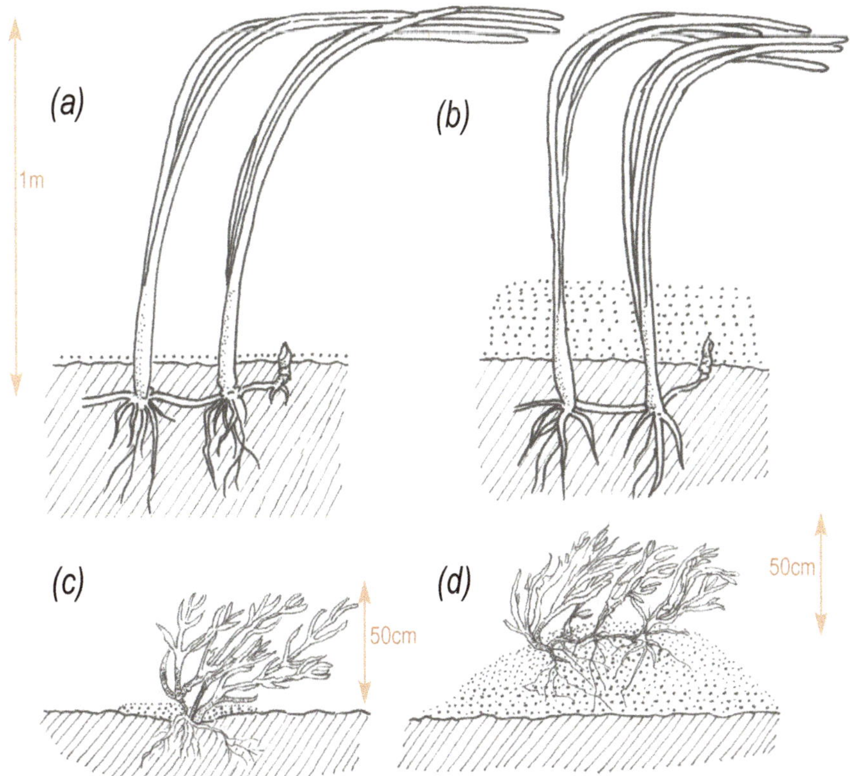

Fig. 25. Effect of sedimentation: (a) and (b) plants with constant rooting level growing well in spite of sedimentation; (c) and (d) plants with a variable rooting level whose roots vary with substrate level. If roots are shallow, as in (d), plants whose roots are only in loose sediment will be washed away in storms.

Fig. 26a. In 2013 where the bridge had stood there was a shallow crossing place for walkers and bikes, but the bed had a silted, gravelly bottom with blanket weed and a few other plants growing near the banks

Fig. 26b. Also 2013, upstream of (a) shows the sprawling Sparganium emersum *right across the river, and (inset) piling up with summer growth amongst the advancing fringing herbs by the bank near a drainage outlet.* Sparganium emersum *came to dominate (Why? This happened over a wide area), then became smaller and other species regrew*

Afterword

When it comes to roots, the study of river plants is more difficult. You would need a site with legal access that bears species you are interested in. Then you have to be able to climb down into the river (and up again, which may be worse!). The water must be deep enough for the specified plants, but not so deep you cannot reach into the water and into the substrate, or so deep that you are working with soaking gum boots. And if any reader is wondering why shoots have been studied so much more than roots, this is most probably the reason!

If you are interested to learn about aquatic plants, including their roots, it is recommended that you get in touch with your local Wildlife or Nature organisation which may have courses which include site visits. This will give you access to a proper site and tuition from a qualified member of staff.

The legalities of the Wildlife and Countryside Act are far too complicated to go into here, especially when it comes to pulling up plants to look at their roots!

Table 1. Trophic nutrient status of rivers (unconsolidated silt) and habitats

TROPHIC STATUS	EXAMPLE OF HABITAT
Dystrophic (nutrient deficient, acid)	Blanket bog • Moor streams Stream sizes up to 4m wide, with water-supported species
Oligotrophic (low nutrient)	Acid sand streams • (semi-infertile) sands streams Stream sizes up to 4m wide, with water-supported species
Mesotrophic (moderate nutrient)	Limestone streams. Stream sizes from 1m to 8m wide Sandstone streams • Clay streams. 4m to 8m wide

---

If you are unfamiliar with the Latin names of the plants listed in Table 2 (overleaf), please visit the Resources section on the River Friend Website where you can download a free screen version of the *Prologue to the Series* (which has illustrations of most of the plants mentioned in this series) for plant identification with English names, a glossary of terms used in the series, and a reference list for further reading.
https://riverfriend.tinasfineart.uk
https://riverfriend.tinasfineart.uk/product/a-prologue-to-the-river-friend-series-isbn-978-1-9162096-2-6/
https://riverfriend.tinasfineart.uk/wp-content/uploads/2020/06/RFS3Revision-June-2020-WEBUSE.pdf

Table 2. Nutrient banding of commoner river species

TROPHIC STATUS	SPECIES*
Dystrophic	*Sphagnum* spp. • *Drosera rotundifolia* • *Drosera anglica* • *Narthecium ossifragum* • *Eriophorum angustifolium* • *Littorella uniflora* • *Menyanthes trifoliata* • *Potamogeton polygonifolius* • *Carex rostrata* • *Ranunculus flammula* • *Sparganium angustifolium*
Dystrophic to Oligotrophic	*Caltha palustris* • *Ranunculus hederaceus* • *Ranunculus omiophyllus* • *Oenanthe crocata* (channel, not bank) • *Myriophyllum alterniflorum* • *Callitriche hamulata* • *Juncus articulatus* • *Eleocharis acicularis* • *Scirpus fluitans* • *Juncus bulbosus* • *Nymphaea alba* (not planted) • *(Nuphar lutea* local, with other from here) • *Eleocharis palustris*
Oligotrophic	*Glyceria fluitans* (with long floating leaves) • *Potamogeton gramineus* • *Potamogeton* × *sparganifolius* • *Carex acuta* (hill) • *Potamogeton alpinus* • *Phalaris arundinacea* • *Iris pseudacorus* (highland) • Mosses (hill) • (*Carex acutiformis* with others from here) • Blanket weed sparse, hills • *Petasites hybridus*
Mesotrophic, limestone and other rocks	*Mimulus guttatus* • *Lemna trisulca* • *Veronica beccabunga* • *Berula erecta* • *Mentha aquatica* • *Ranunculus* (short leaved, Batrachian) • *Callitriche* spp. (not *C. hamulata*) • Mosses, lowlands • *Nasturtium officinale* agg. • *Ranunculus* (medium leaved, Batrachian) • *Solanum dulcamara* • *Apium nodiflorum* • *Myosotis scorpioides* • *(Oenanthe crocata,* banks) • *Veronica anagallis-aquatica* agg. • *Potamogeton natans* • *Hippuris vulgaris* • *Ranunculus trichophyllus* • *Sparganium erectum*
Semi-eutrophic (moderate to high nutrient)	*Elodea canadensis* • *Carex acutiformis* agg. • *Phragmites australis* • *Potamogeton perfoliatus* • *Ranunculus penicillatus,* long-leaved • *Polygonum amphibium* • Blanket weed • *Groenlandia densa* • *Zannichellia palustris* • *Oenanthe fluviatilis* • *Ranunculus fluitans* • *Glyceria maxima* • *Alisma plantago-aquatica* • *(Nymphaea alba* former clay stream position) • *Potamogeton lucens* • *Myriophyllum spicatum* • *Acorus calamus* (introduced) • *Potamogeton crispus* • *Phalaris arundinacea* • *Iris pseudacorus* (lowland)
Eutrophic (high nutrient)	*Epilobium hirsutum* • (*Caltha palustris,* just on bank—often planted) • *Enteromorpha* sp. • *Ceratophyllum demersum* • *Rumex hydrolapathum* • *Sparganium emersum* • *Sagittaria sagittifolia* • *Butomus umbellatus* • *Potamogeton pectinatus* • *Rorippa amphibia* • *Scirpus lacustris* • *Nuphar lutea*
Non-banded	*Agrostis stolonifera* and other small grasses not listed above • *Lemna minor* agg. • Other and rare aquatics (many of which can be banded by detailed study in their habitats) • Land species

CITATIONS

Butcher, R.W., for example, "A preliminary account of the vegetation of the River Itchen". *Journal of Ecology,* Vol. 15, pp. 55–65 (1927).

Haslam, S.M. (1987). *River Plants of Western Europe.* Cambridge University Press. 512 pp. ISBN 0-521-26427-8. Also other books by her, **see website: https://riversandreeds.co.uk**.

Haslam, S.M., MA, ScD. (1997). *The River Scene: Ecology and Cultural Heritage*, available from Amazon and other leading bookshops (Hardback and Paperback) Cambridge University Press. ISBN-13-978-0521574105.

Rumsfeld, D.H. (2002). Quotation from *United States Government Defense News Transcript*: DoD News Briefing—Secretary Rumsfeld and General Myers, United States Department of Defense. Presenter: Secretary of Defense Donald H. Rumsfeld. February 12, 2002. Source, Wikipedia: URL: https://en.wikipedia.org/wiki/There_are_known_knowns [accessed July 2022].

THE RIVER FRIEND SERIES

This series of small books is designed for people with a general or specific interest in rivers.
Please visit the River Friend Website for an up to-date list of
PUBLISHED Titles: **http://www.riverfriend.tinasfineart.uk**

Standalone* Titles in the Series include:

A PROLOGUE TO THE SERIES: Plant identification and Glossary of Terms (ISBN 978 1 9162096 2 6)

DRYING UP (ISBN 978 1 9162096 1 9)

STREAM STORY I: A Riveting Riverscape—River Brue, Somerset (ISBN 978 1 9162096 0 2)

INTERPRET: What do Plants Tell us? (ISBN 978 1 9162096 5 7)

REED—ON THE EDGE (ISBN 978 1 9162096 4 0)

An Introduction to the WATER FRAMEWORK DIRECTIVE (ISBN 978 1 9162096 3 3)

WATER: Clean and Dirty **(ISBN 978 1 9162096 7 1)**

STREAM STORY: A Brook in Transit: Bourn Brook, Cambridge (ISBN 978 1 9162096 8 8)

Vegetation Changes Over Time. Is there FREEZE FRAME? (ISBN 978 1 9162096 6 4)

AWFUL ALIENS: Foreign Plants of the River and its Banks

WHAT RIVERS DO FOR US

STREAM STORY: Another Riveting Riverscape—River Cam, Cambridge

LOOK AT THE BOTTOM

*Each book is about a different subject so the series can be read in any order

About the Authors

Sylvia Haslam is a botanist and river culture, etc., specialist. Anyone wanting to find out more should look at the publications list on her website (**https://www.riversandreeds.co.uk**). Her publications specific to this series are listed in the book entitled *A PROLOGUE TO THE SERIES: Plant identification and Glossary of Terms.*

Tina Bone has worked as a self-employed Desktop Publisher for many years until she changed career to work as a Professional Artist and Book Publisher from March 2005. To view Tina's résumé and artwork please visit her website: https://www.tinasfineart.uk.